W9-BQT-172

JOHN THOMPSON'S MODERN COURSE FOR THE PIANO

TEACHING LITTLE FINGERS TO PLAY

NOTE TO PARENTS

This is your child's FIRST PIANO BOOK.

As a parent you have a right to expect progress. If you will assist the teacher by arousing your child's interest and enthusiasm in each successive lesson, the result will speak for itself.

Words have been added to most of the musical examples to help interpret the spirit of the little melodies. So READ THEM to the youngster and EXPLAIN their meaning. These melodies were written with careful thought and were kept as simple as possible in order to keep them within the grasp of a child's hand, which is quite naturally, small. Help the student play in strict time. Even if you do not play piano yourself, it will be fun.

DUET PLAYING FOR PARENT AND PUPIL

Parents who play the piano even a little are advised to examine a supplementary book to "TEACHING LITTLE FINGERS TO PLAY," called "TEACHING LITTLE FINGERS TO PLAY ENSEMBLE." This is a separate book containing duet-accompaniments that have been arranged to supply the harmonies for use with each little melody found in "TEACHING LITTLE FINGERS TO PLAY." By using the supplementary book, parents or teacher may play DUETS with the child from the very beginning. The attractiveness of playing with someone else is very strong to any young beginner who finds the study of piano a bit lonesome at the start. It is also one of the most delightful means of enjoying music in the home and, incidentally, develops strict observance of rhythm and quick thinking.

Psychologists claim that the hazard of loneliness in piano study is a very real one, and "TEACHING LITTLE FINGERS TO PLAY ENSEMBLE" banishes this obstacle to the happy progress of the child.

Ask your teacher or music dealer to show you the book called "TEACHING LITTLE FINGERS TO PLAY ENSEMBLE".

THE WILLIS MUSIC COMPANY **FLORENCE, KENTUCKY 41042**

Cover, Design & Illustrations By Nicholas E. Gressle ©1994

TO THE TEACHER

HOW TO PRESENT THE FIRST THREE LESSONS IN *TEACHING LITTLE FINGERS TO PLAY*

When children can place their tiny fingers on the piano keyboard and PLAY A TUNE during the first few moments of their first lesson they discover that to learn music is as easy as any play-time activity. Hence, the advisability of TEACHING BY ROTE.

This book incorporates rote teaching, the ADVANTAGE of this being that the pupil cheerfully makes music while simultaneously mastering the necessary rudiments required to PLAY BY NOTE.

The following procedure, if carefully observed, will teach any pupil to MAKE MUSIC FIVE MINUTES after the first lesson, and by the fourth lesson the pupil will be able to PLAY BY NOTE.

FIRST LESSON

The musical examples in the first three lessons are to be taught ENTIRELY BY ROTE (i.e., imitation). The purpose is to teach the NAMES OF THE KEYS ONLY. The notes will be learned later.

1. Teach *Stepping* and *Skipping*, first as a song. The teacher plays and sings a few times until the pupil memorizes both TUNE and WORDS. (The pupil is already making music.)
When the pupil can SING it correctly, teach him to PLAY it on the piano by *finger patterns*.

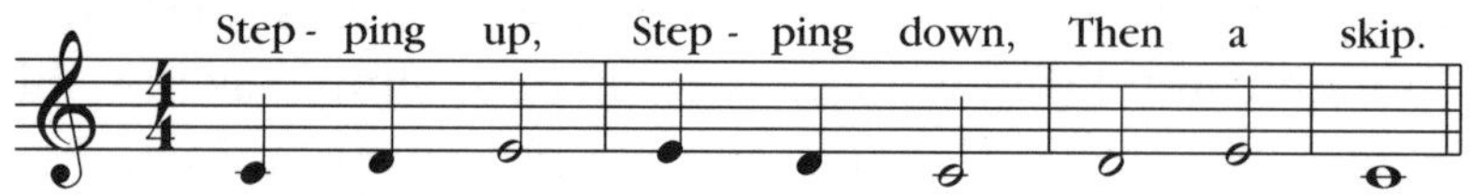
Step - ping up, Step - ping down, Then a skip.

2. Teach the *number names* of the fingers.

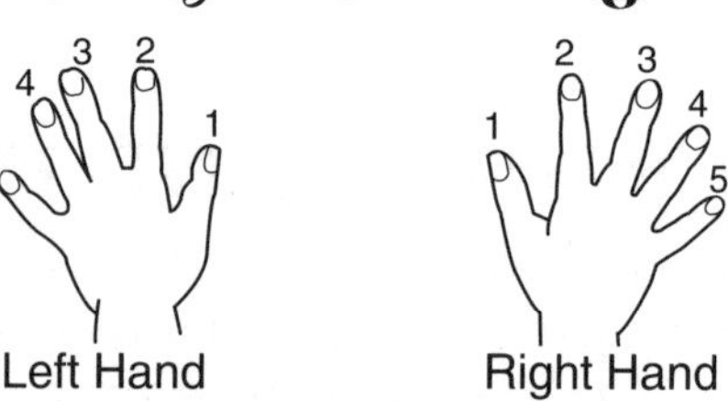
Left Hand
Right Hand

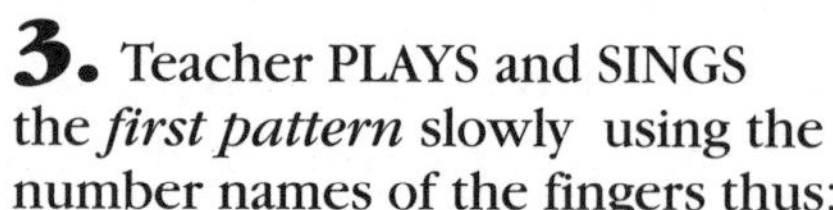

3. Teacher PLAYS and SINGS the *first pattern* slowly using the number names of the fingers thus:

FIRST PATTERN

SING: ONE TWO THREE

4. When the pupil can *imitate* the first pattern, PLAY and SING the second pattern the same way and have the pupil imitate.

SECOND PATTERN

SING: THREE TWO ONE

5. Now PLAY and SING the *third pattern* and have the pupil imitate in exactly the same way.

THIRD PATTERN

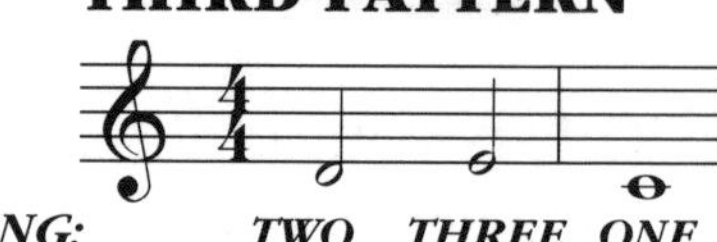
SING: TWO THREE ONE

6. When the pupil can play all three patterns using the number names of the fingers, then teach him or her to play and sing the *letter names of the keys*:

SING: C D E E D C D E C
PLAY:

7. After the pupil has played the three patterns, first with the RIGHT HAND and then with the LEFT HAND ALONE, he or she should be instructed to play them in different octaves on the keyboard; see example below.

RIGHT HAND
SING: C D E E D C D E C

LEFT HAND
SING: C D E E D C D E C

TO THE TEACHER (Continued)

The pupil has sung and played a tune in much less time than it has taken to describe. He or she has played with the LEFT and RIGHT hands and developed the first three fingers of each hand equally.

THE PUPIL HAS LEARNED TO RECOGNIZE AND PLAY THREE KEYS ON THE KEYBOARD

THE LESSON IN NOTATION

The first lesson is very simple. The pupil is taught to recognize the TREBLE and BASS CLEF signs, BAR LINES and MEASURES as illustrated on page 5. Teachers usually have individual methods for teaching the rudiments; hence, all examples are subject to the effect of a suggestion — the success of your own individuality.

SECOND LESSON

Proceed exactly as in Lesson One. First as a SONG, then by FINGER PATTERNS (*pupil singing number names of fingers*). Finally as shown in example (*pupil now singing letter names of keys*).
After the pupil can play the example with each hand separately in various octaves COMBINE GROUPS 2 and 1 as follows:

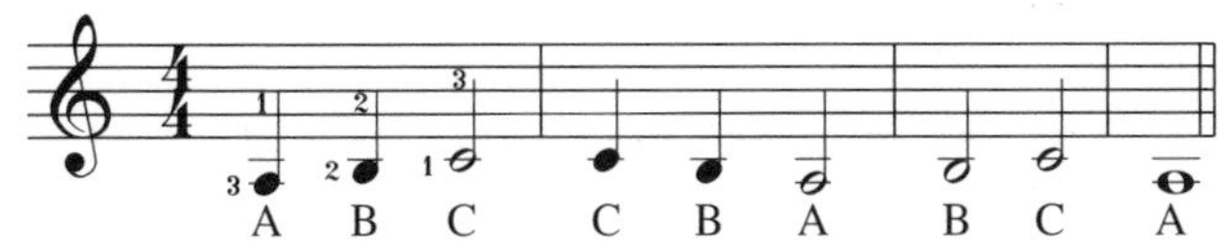
A B C C B A B C A

SING:

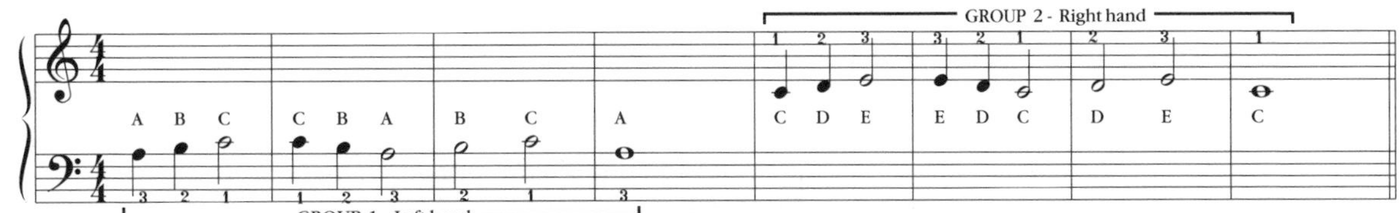
GROUP 2 - Right hand
A B C C B A B C A
C D E E D C D E C
GROUP 1 - Left hand

The pupil has learned FIVE keys on the keyboard — A B C D E — and can PLAY and SING a tune of 8 measures, using both hands.

THE LESSON IN NOTATION

In this second lesson, the pupil is taught to recognize and know the value of QUARTER-NOTES, HALF- and WHOLE - NOTES.
(The quarter - note is used as a unit instead of the whole - note to avoid fractions. "ONE NOTE, ONE COUNT," is easily understood,whereas when the whole - note is taught first, the child is asked to *divide a note in his* mind into four fractional parts.)

THIRD LESSON

Teach the remaining letter - names E F G by presenting Stepping and Skipping on the new keys as in other lessons.
When the example can be played with either hand in various octaves COMBINE GROUPS 3 and 1 as follows:

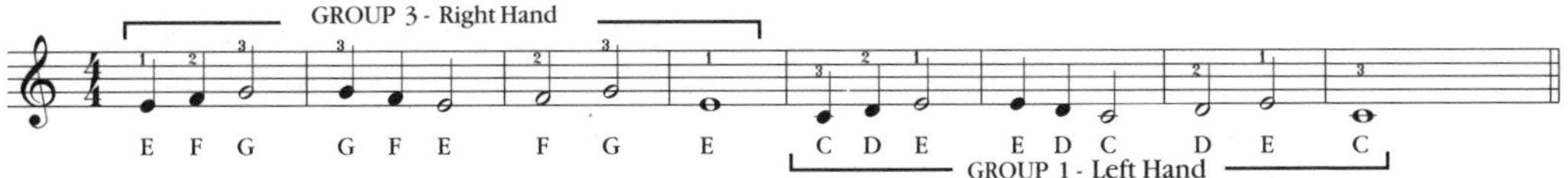
GROUP 3 - Right Hand
E F G G F E F G E
C D E E D C D E C
GROUP 1 - Left Hand

The pupil now learns TIME SIGNATURES in the LESSON IN NOTATION (pg. 7).
He has learned all 7 white keys — A B C D E F G, has been making music for three lessons and has absorbed enough knowledge of NOTATION to enable him or her to read without dictation from now on. Thus ROTE TEACHING has been used as a MEANS TOWARD AN END.

(NOTE: — After the third lesson, material should be assigned according to the capacity of each individual pupil)

Contents

"Something New Every Lesson"

To the Teacher 2
First Keyboard and Notation Lesson *(Rote)* 5
Second Keyboard and Notation Lesson *(Rote)* 6
Third Keyboard and Notation Lesson *(Rote)* 7
Correlating Keys and Notes *(C,D,E)* — "The Birthday Party" 8
Correlating Keys and Notes *(A,B,C)* — "Sandman's Near" 9
Two Notes in Both Directions from Middle C *(2/4) time)* — "Baseball Days" 10
Three Notes in Both Directions from Middle C *(Dotted half-note 3/4 time)* — "The Postman" 11
Four - Four Time — "Rain on the Roof" 12
Dotted Half-note in 4/4 Time *(A minor)* — "Song of the Volga Boatmen" 13
Musical Sentences called Phrases — "A Message" 14
Four Notes in Both Directions from Middle C— "Chimes" 15
The Tale of a Famous Carol — "Good King Wenceslas" 16
Signs of Silence called Rests — "Lazy Mary" 17
Cross-Hand — "Betty and Bill" 18
Time Value of Eighth Notes — "Flying to the Moon" 19
Skipping a White Key *(3rd's)* — "Air, from Surprise Symphony" 20
Introducing Bass Notes C and G *(an octave below Middle C)* — "By the Pond" 21
The Black Key Sign called Sharp — "Paper Ships" 22
F Sharp in the Key Signature — "Sledding" 23
Second Recreation in the Key of G *(the Tie)* "The Butterfly" 24
Introducing Treble Notes *(an octave above Middle C)* — "Questions" 25
Middle C Sharp *(Accidental)* — "Blue Bells of Scotland" 26
Skipping White Keys *(Triad)* — "Toy Soldiers" 27
A Few Measures with Two Hands Together — "Big Ships" 28
The Flat and Accidental Signs — "Steamboat 'round the Bend" 29
B♭ in the Key Signature — "Comin Round the Mountain" *(Duet)* 30-31
Cross-Hand — "The Long Trail" 32
An Accidental *(A sharp)* — "The Bee" 33
Beginning on a Weak Beat — "My Bonnie" 34
Using the 8····· Sign — "Vacation Time" 35
Expression — "Home on the Range" *(Duet)* 36-37
Cross-hand — R.H. and L.H. — "The Juggler" 38
Two Notes Together *(Chord)* — "From a Wigwam" 39
Certificate of Merit 40

Teachers who, for the sake of thoroughness, desire to have the pupil practice writing BAR LINES, CLEFS, TIME SIGNATURES, etc., etc., will find "JOHN THOMPSON'S NOTE SPELLER" very useful. — J.T.

FIRST LESSON AT THE KEYBOARD

LEARNING THE KEYS **C D E**

The **BLACK** keys of the piano keyboard are divided into patterns of **TWO** and **THREE**. To the left of the TWO **BLACK** key pattern, in the center of your piano under the maker's name, is **MIDDLE C.**

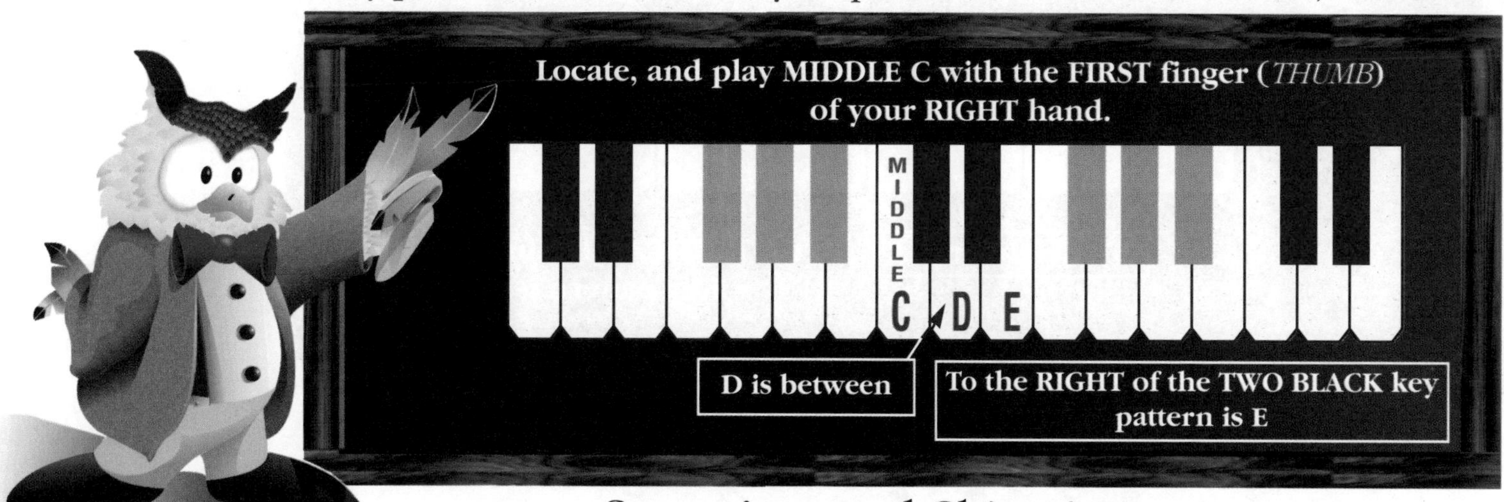
Locate, and play MIDDLE C with the FIRST finger (THUMB) of your RIGHT hand.
MIDDLE
C
D
E
D is between
To the RIGHT of the TWO BLACK key pattern is E

Stepping and Skipping

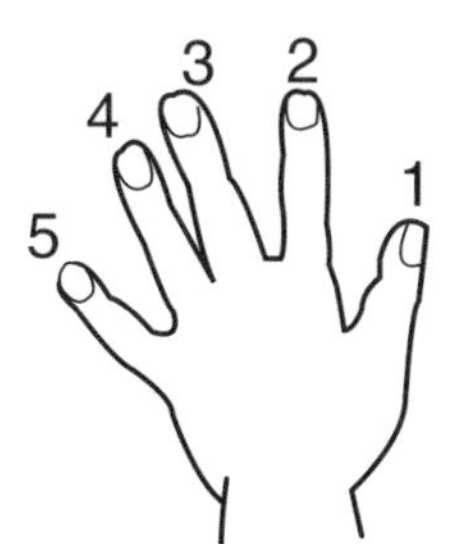
5
4
3
2
1

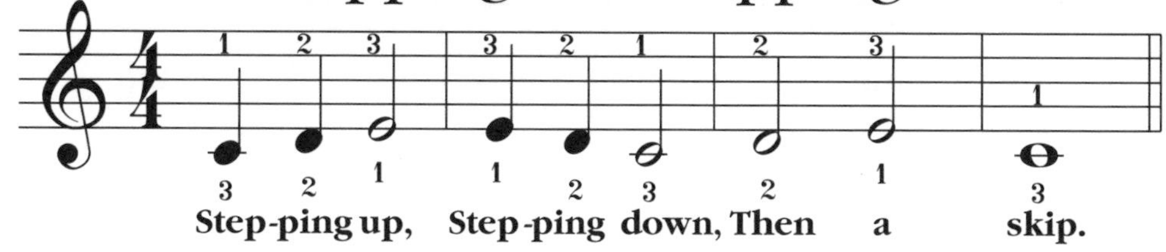
Step-ping up, Step-ping down, Then a skip.

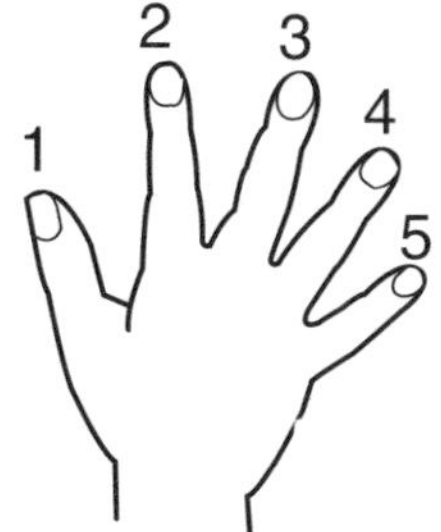
1
2
3
4
5

(1) Learn first as a SONG. **(2)** PLAY and SING the words. **(3)** Play and sing the letter-names of the KEYS. **(4)** Play each hand separately in VARIOUS OCTAVES

LEFT HAND **RIGHT HAND**

FIRST LESSON IN NOTATION

Learning the Grand Staff, Clef Signs, Bars and Measures

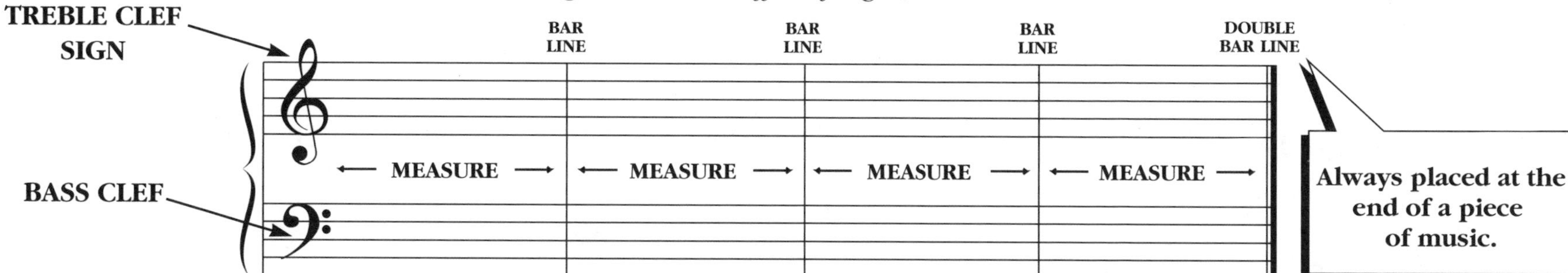
TREBLE CLEF SIGN
BASS CLEF
BAR LINE
BAR LINE
BAR LINE
DOUBLE BAR LINE
MEASURE
MEASURE
MEASURE
MEASURE
Always placed at the end of a piece of music.

SECOND LESSON AT THE KEYBOARD

NEW KEYS A, B, and playing A B C
MIDDLE
A B C
B's neighbor is A
To the RIGHT of the three BLACK Key pattern is B

Always
Be
Curious
to find other A, B, C's on the keyboard

Stepping and Skipping from A

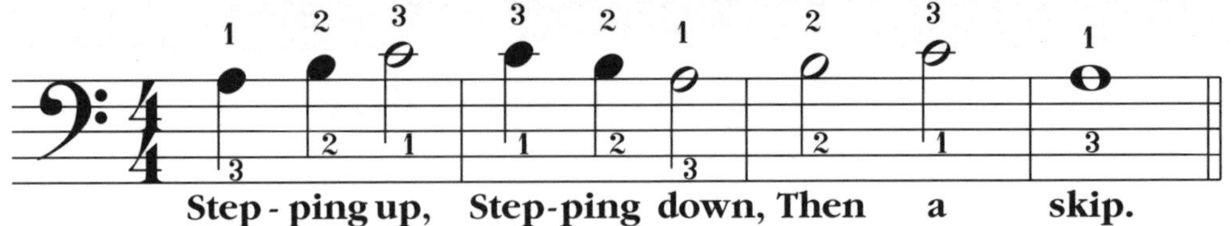
1 2 3 3 2 1 2 3 1
3 2 1 1 2 3 2 1 3
Step - ping up, Step-ping down, Then a skip.

Combining Group 2 and Group 1

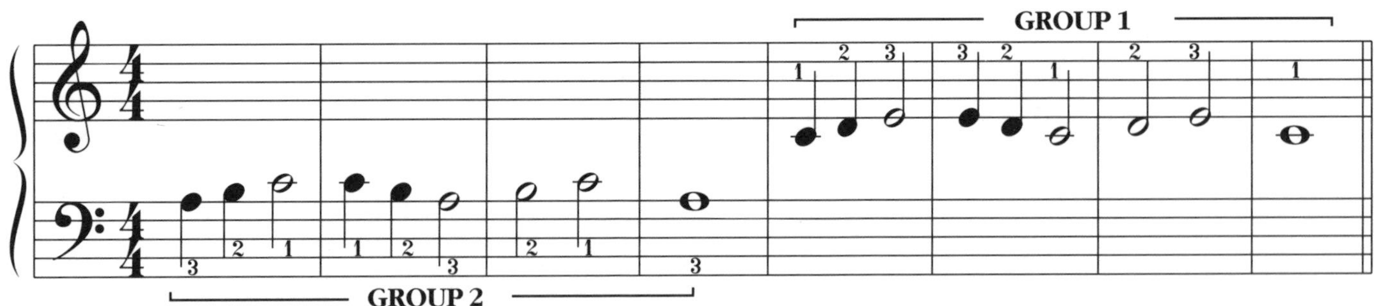
GROUP 1
1 2 3 3 2 1 2 3 1
3 2 1 1 2 3 2 1 3
GROUP 2

SECOND LESSON IN NOTATION:

Notes, like Coins, have different values

A **QUARTER - NOTE** IS HELD FOR **1 COUNT**

A **HALF - NOTE** IS HELD FOR **2 COUNTS**

A **WHOLE - NOTE** IS HELD FOR **4 COUNTS**

THIRD LESSON AT THE KEYBOARD

New Keys F, G and playing E F G
MIDDLE C
F G
To the LEFT of the three BLACK Key pattern is F
F's neighbor is G

Always
Be
Curious
to find other E, F, G's on the keyboard

Stepping and Skipping from E

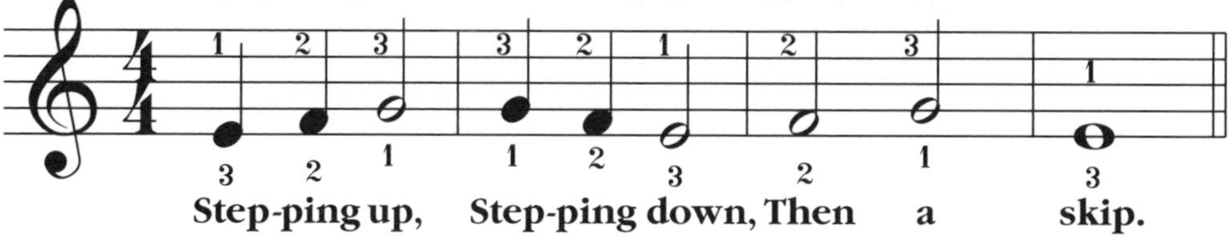
Step-ping up, Step-ping down, Then a skip.

Combining Group 3 and 1

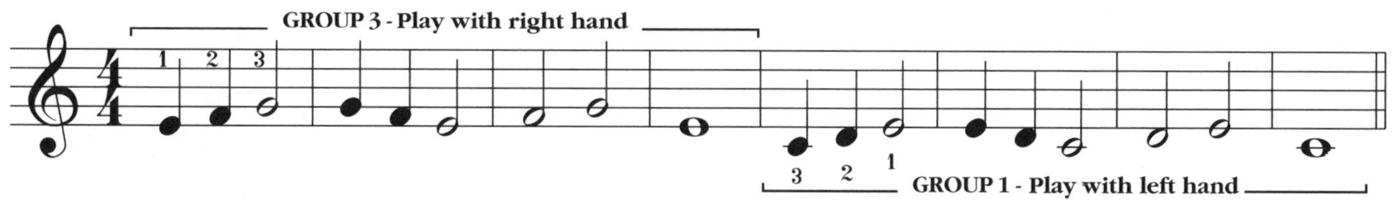
GROUP 3 - Play with right hand
GROUP 1 - Play with left hand

THIRD LESSON IN NOTATION

The TIME SIGNATURE next to the CLEF sign at the beginning of a piece tells us how it should be counted.

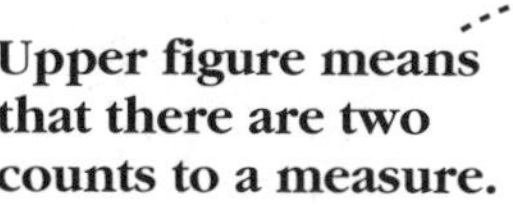

Upper figure means that there are two counts to a measure.

Lower figure means that each quarter-note gets one count.

Count: 1 2 1 2

THREE Counts to a measure.

Quarter-Note gets one count.

Count: 1 2 3 1 2 3

FOUR counts to a measure.

Quarter Note gets one count.

Count: 1 2 3 4 1 2 3 4 1234

Birthday Party

1/2
♩=60 / ♩=80

1

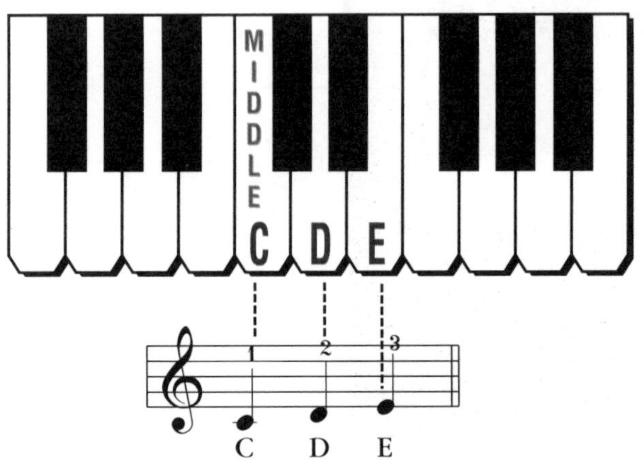
MIDDLE
C D E
1 2 3
C D E

Right hand GROUP for this piece.
Locate C D E in other parts of keyboard

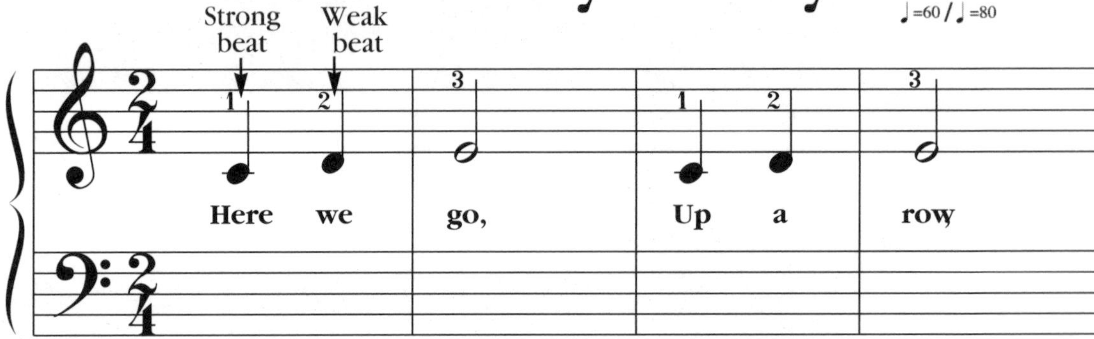
Strong beat
Weak beat
1 2 3 1 2 3
Here we go,
Up a row

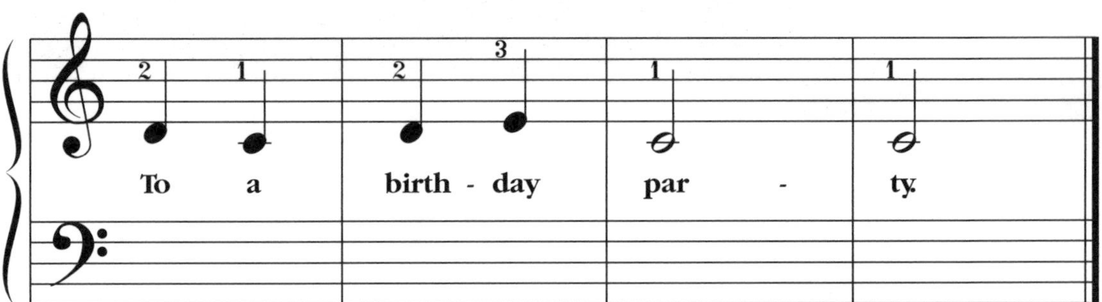
2 1 2 3 1 1
To a birth - day par - ty.

Left hand GROUP for this piece.
Locate and play A B C in other parts of the keyboard.

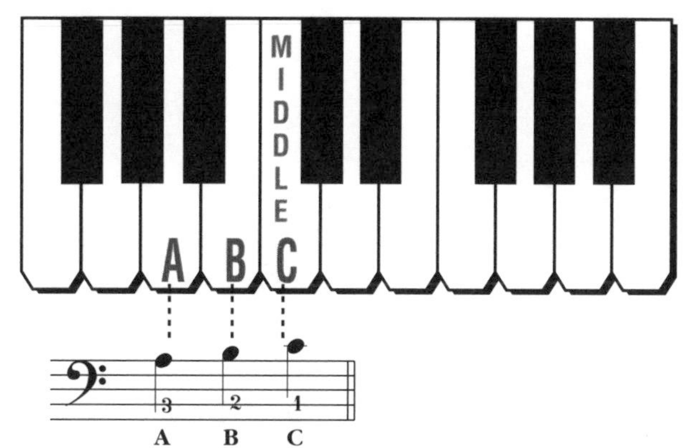
MIDDLE
A B C
3 2 1
A B C

Sandman's Near

3 / 4
♩=60 / ♩=80

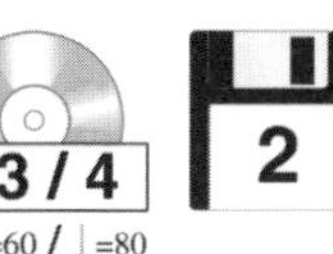
2

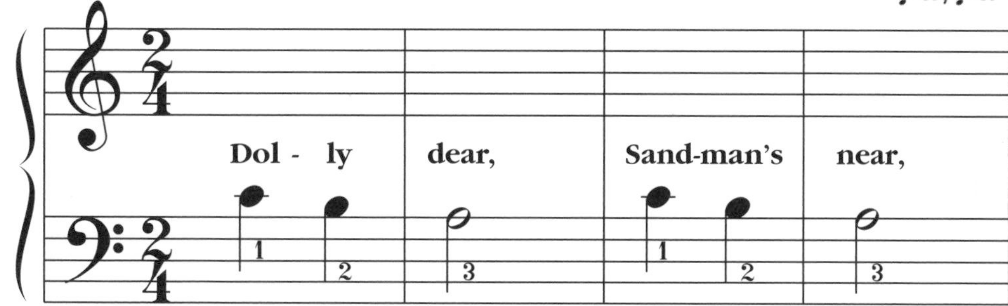
Dol - ly dear, Sand-man's near,
1 2 3 1 2 3

You will soon be sleep - ing.
2 1 2 1 3 3

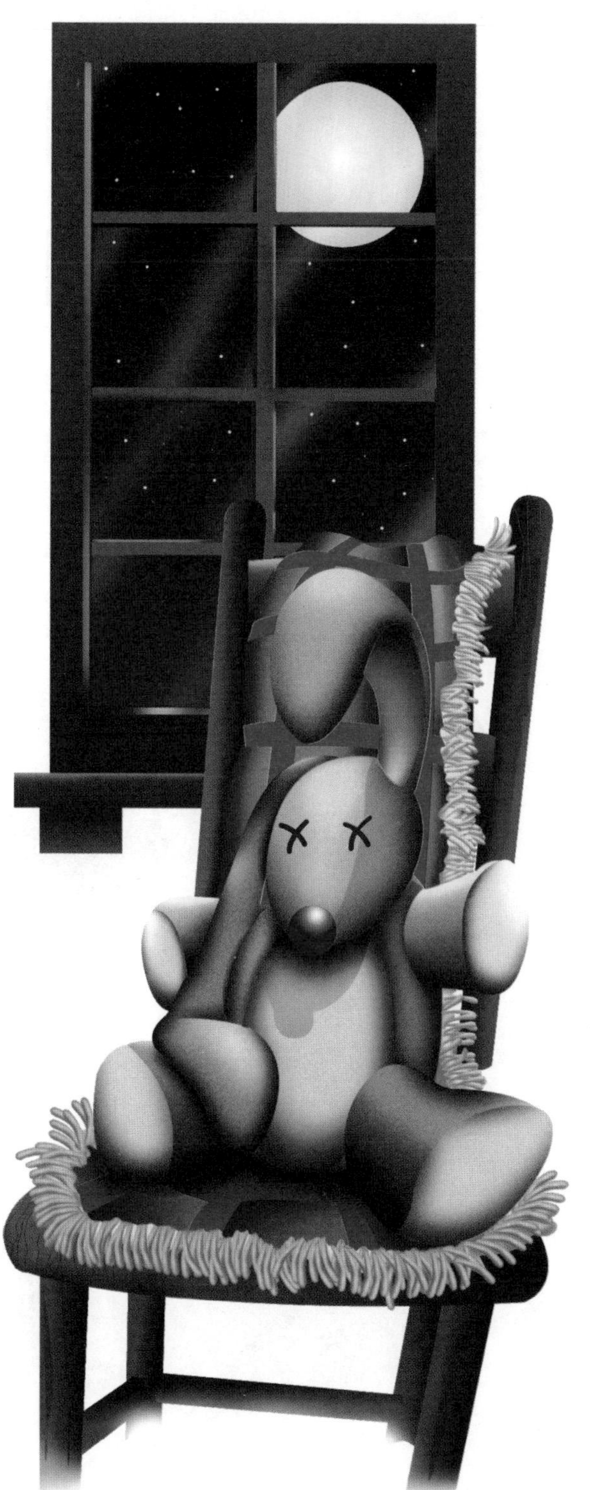

Baseball Days

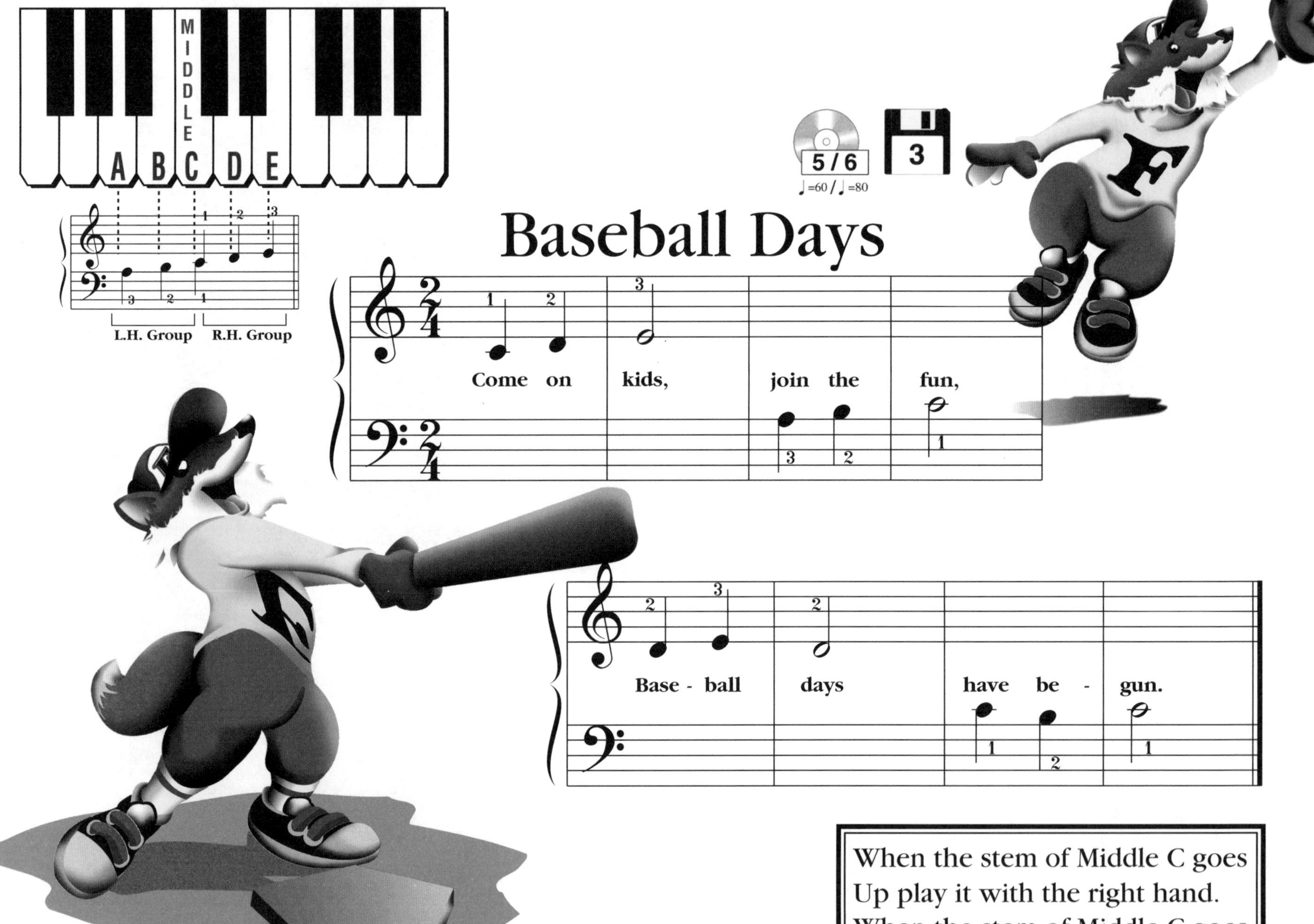
M
I
D
D
L
E
A B C D E
L.H. Group
R.H. Group
5 / 6
♩=60 / ♩=80
3
Come on kids, join the fun,
Base - ball days have be - gun.

When the stem of Middle C goes
Up play it with the right hand.
When the stem of Middle C goes
Down play it with the left hand.

To: Bob Bunny
1 Forest way
The woods 2340-765

Upper figure means that there are 3 counts in each measure.

Lower figure means that each quarter note gets one count.

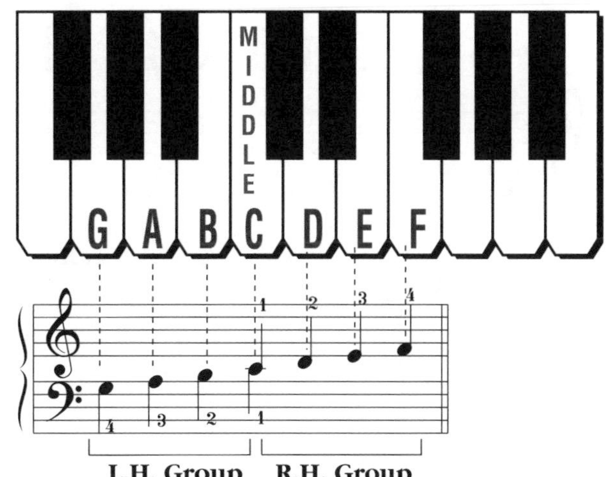
MIDDLE
G A B C D E F
L.H. Group
R.H. Group

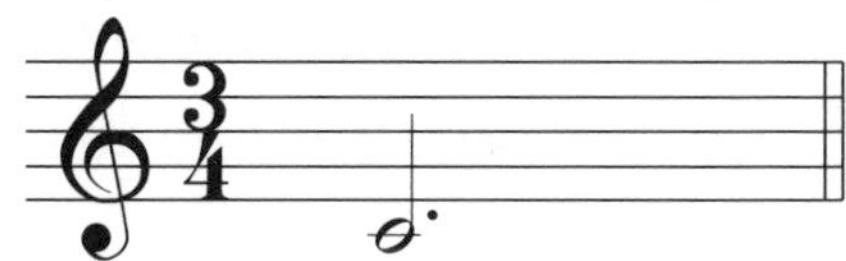

THE DOTTED HALF-NOTE
(THREE-BEAT NOTE)

HOLD 3 BEATS (1,2,3).
A DOT after a note increases its value half the value of the note before it.

The Postman

7/8
♩=60 / ♩=80

4

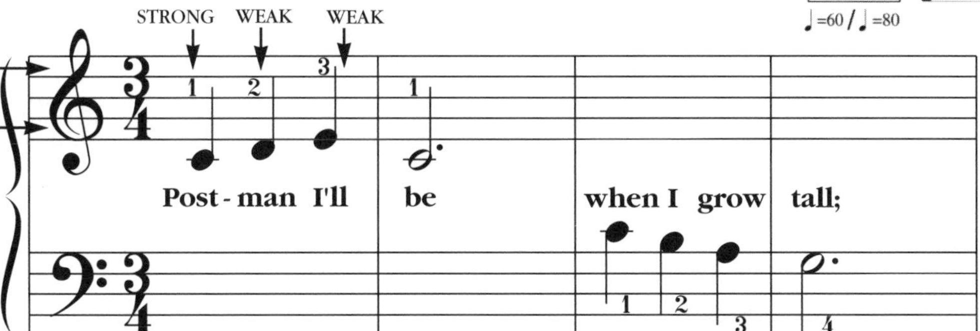
STRONG
WEAK
WEAK
Post - man I'll
be
when I grow
tall;

Let - ters I'll
bring you in
win - ter and
fall.

In 3-4 Time be sure to accent the first beat of each measure.

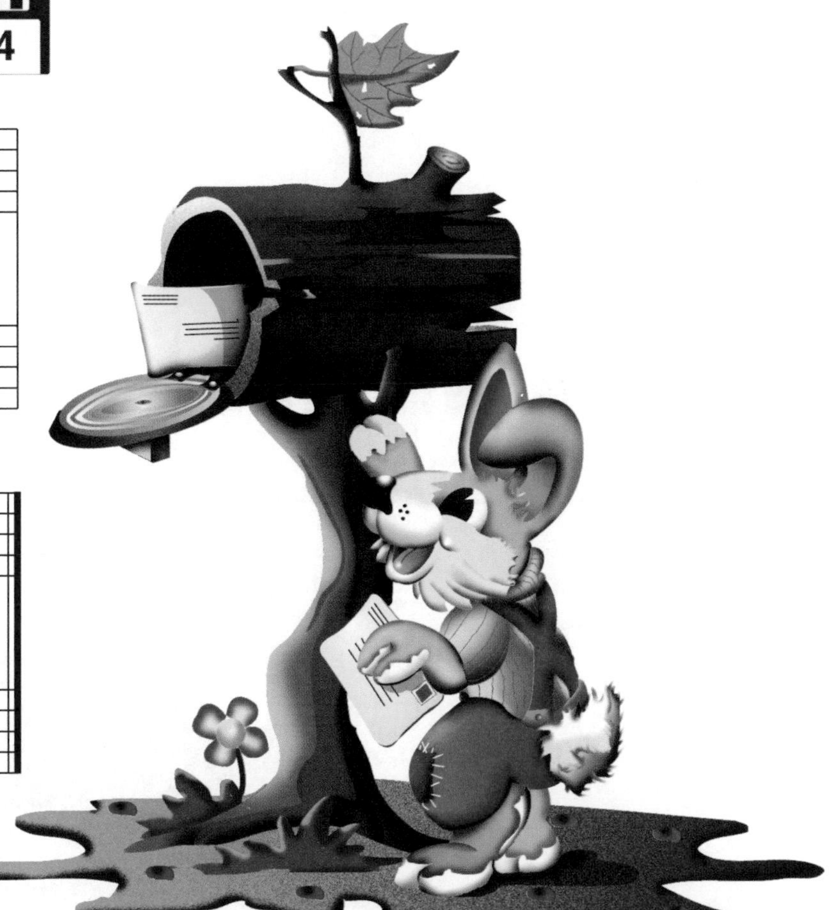

Rain on the Roof

9 / 10
♩=60 / ♩=80

5

4 Counts to each measure.
Quarter Note gets one count.

4/4 Time has one strong beat and three weak beats.

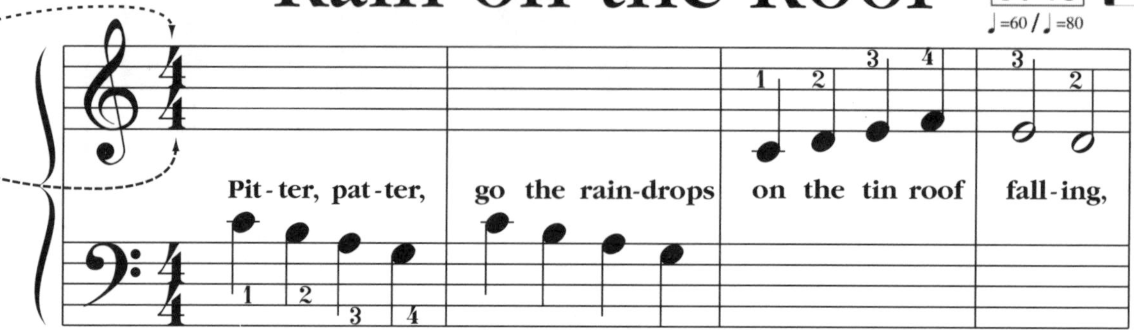
Pit - ter, pat - ter, go the rain-drops on the tin roof fall - ing,

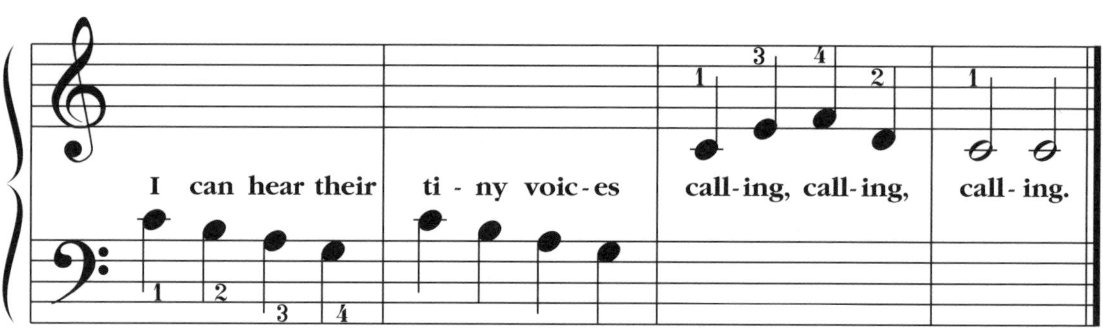
I can hear their ti - ny voic - es call - ing, call - ing, call - ing.

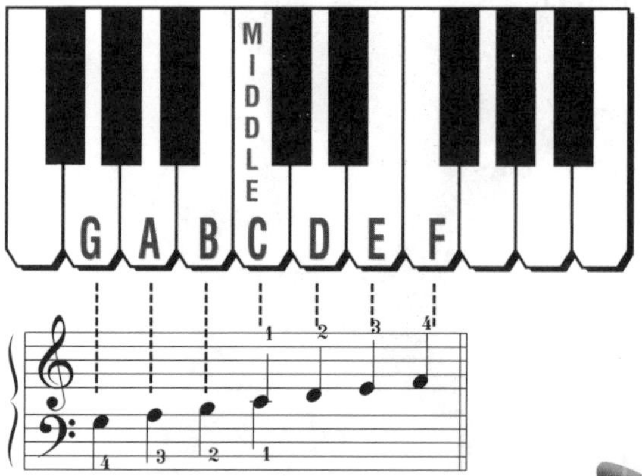

Mark the Left hand and Right hand GROUPS yourself.

1 / 12 6

♩=60 / ♩=80

The Dotted Half Note
𝅗𝅥. In Four–Four Time.

Song of the Volga Boatmen

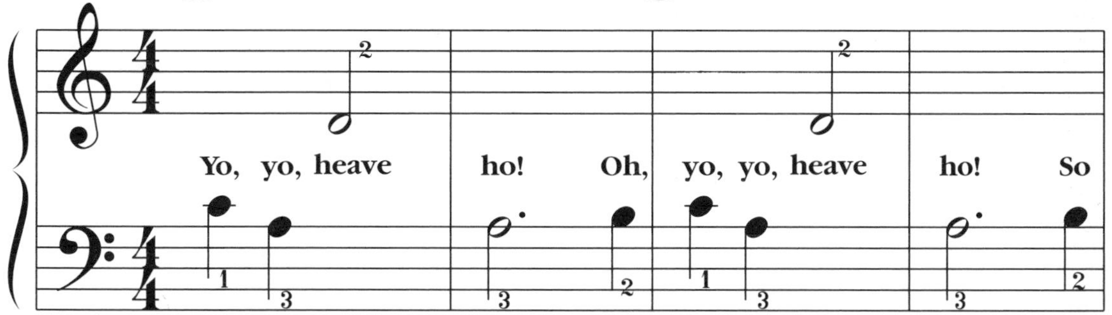

Yo, yo, heave ho! Oh, yo, yo, heave ho! So

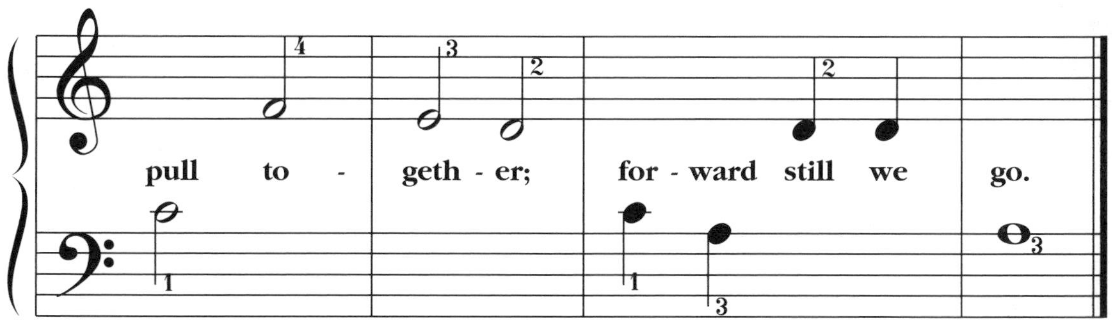

pull to - geth - er; for - ward still we go.

Music is written in HAPPY KEYS (*Major*) and SAD keys (*Minor*).

This famous Russian Folk-Song is an example in a SAD key.

Years ago, before there were steamboats, the peasants who lived along the banks of the Volga used to pull boats and barges, heavily loaded with merchandise, up the river from one village to the next.

The plodding along the banks of those condemned to this labor was terrible. While struggling along they used to lighten their burden by singing the sad strains of this rhythmical melody.

Groups of notes, like words in books,
tell stories when arranged in sentences
and punctuated.
A curved line over groups of notes indicates
MUSICAL SENTENCES called PHRASES.

MIDDLE
G
C
G
L.H. Group
R.H. Group

A Message

13 / 14
♩=65 / ♩=85
7

English Folk-Tune

Tap, tap, tap, tap, someone's knock-ing at my door to bring a let- ter,
Tap, tap, tap, tap, I wish they'd ring; Our bell sounds much bet- ter.

F
MIDDLE C
G
L.H. Group
R.H. Group
Chimes
15 / 16
♩=60 / ♩=80
8
Ding dong, dong ding
Hear the chimes ring;
From the high tow'r,
Hark to the hour.
ONE
TWO
THREE
FOUR.

17 / 18
9
♩=63 / ♩=83

Good King Wenceslas

THIS very ancient tune was a great favorite among the carol singers who used to beg for alms many centuries ago. It is based on the legend of King Wenceslas,the Holy, who was king of Bohemia in the Tenth Century.

On the Feast of St. Stephen (Dec. 26) this good king went out among the poor and gave liberally.

English Christmas Carol

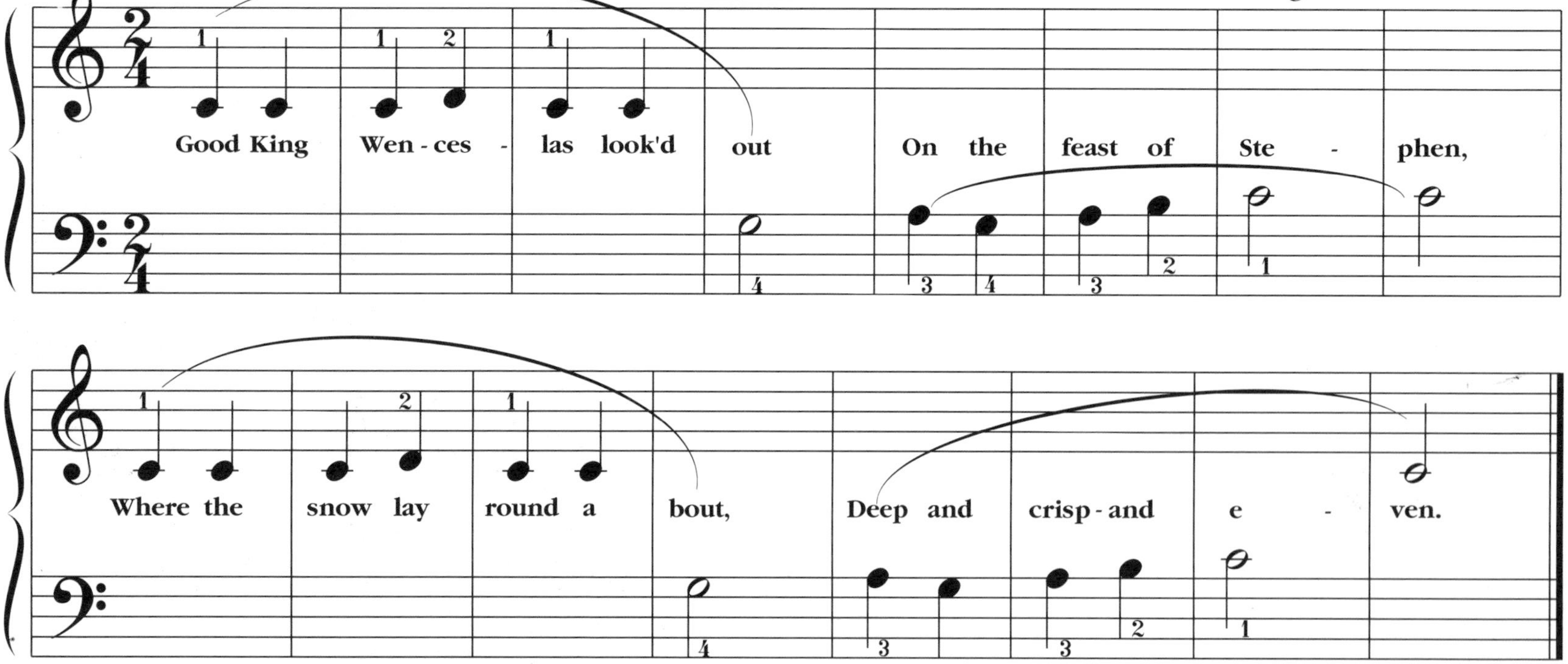

Good King Wen - ces - las look'd out On the feast of Ste - phen,

Where the snow lay round a bout, Deep and crisp - and e - ven.

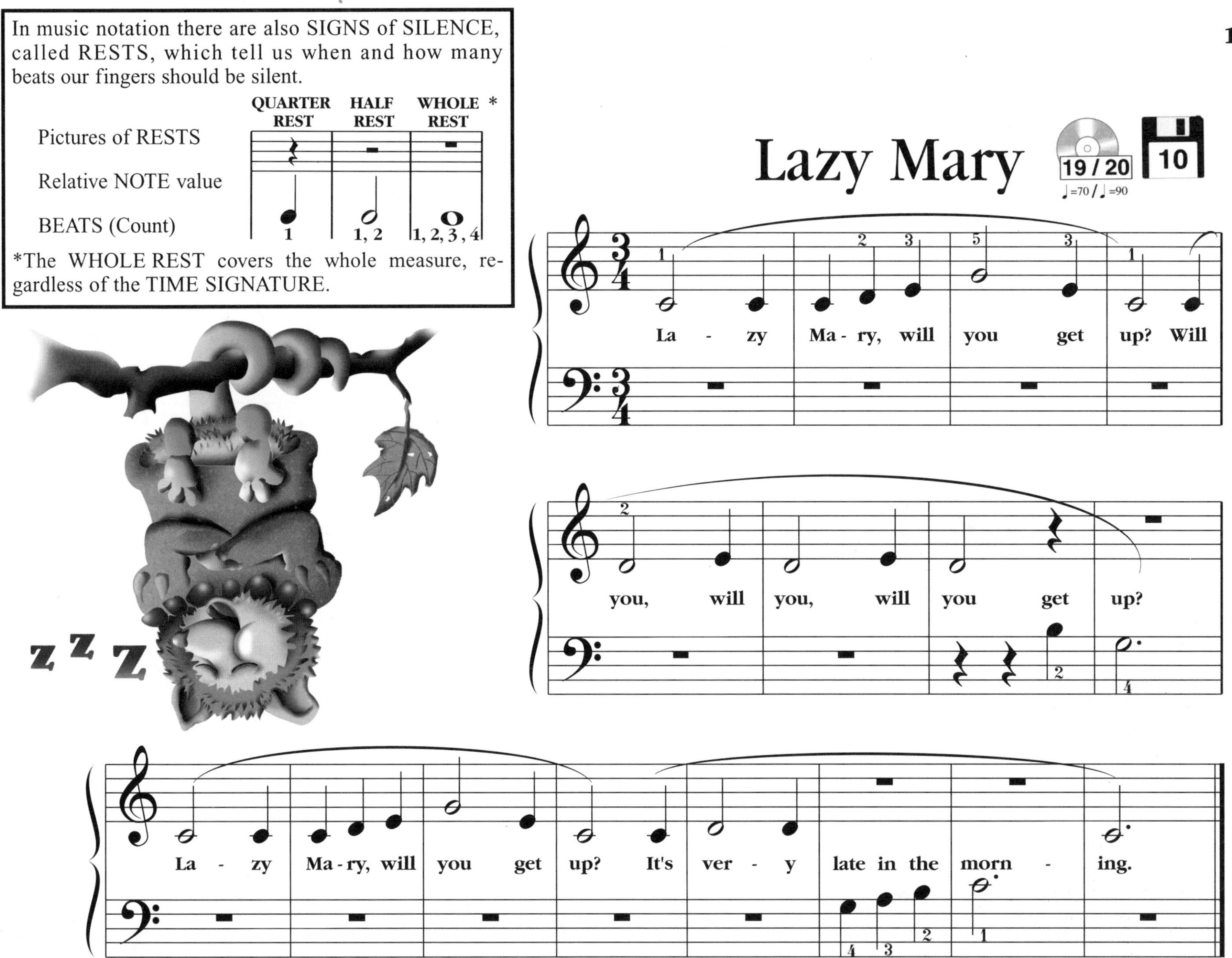
In music notation there are also SIGNS of SILENCE, called RESTS, which tell us when and how many beats our fingers should be silent.
QUARTER REST
HALF REST
WHOLE REST *
Pictures of RESTS
Relative NOTE value
BEATS (Count)
1
1, 2
1, 2, 3, 4
*The WHOLE REST covers the whole measure, regardless of the TIME SIGNATURE.
Lazy Mary
19 / 20
10
♩=70 / ♩=90
La - zy Ma - ry, will you get up? Will
you, will you, will you get up?
La - zy Ma - ry, will you get up? It's ver - y late in the morn - ing.
Z Z Z

READ and name the four notes above and three notes below MIDDLE C. Count as you play.

MIDDLE
G
C
G
C
L.H. Group
R.H. Group
L.H. cross over R.H.
Betty and Bill
21 / 22
11
♩=65 / ♩=85
Gal - lop - ing, gal - lop - ing o - ver the hill,
O, what a frol - ic for L.H. Bet - ty and Bill.
L.H. over

Flying to the Moon

23 / 24 ♩=62 / ♩=82 12

American Folk Tune
(Adapted)

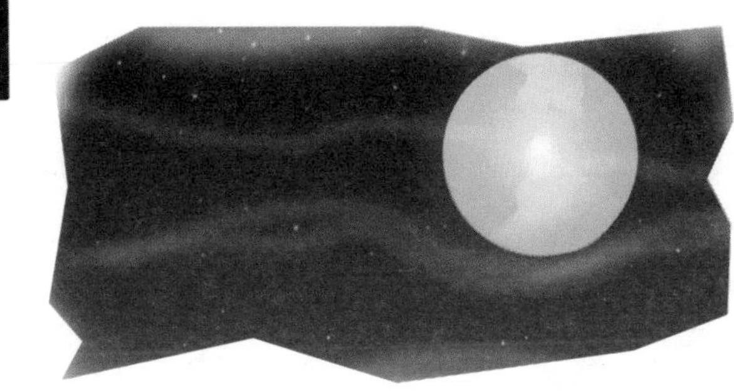

Shall we go a - fly - ing, fly - ing, fly - ing?

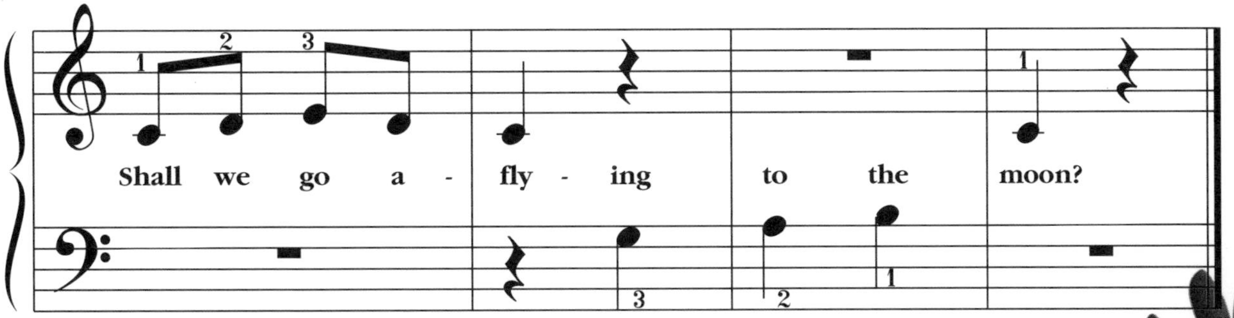

Shall we go a - fly - ing to the moon?

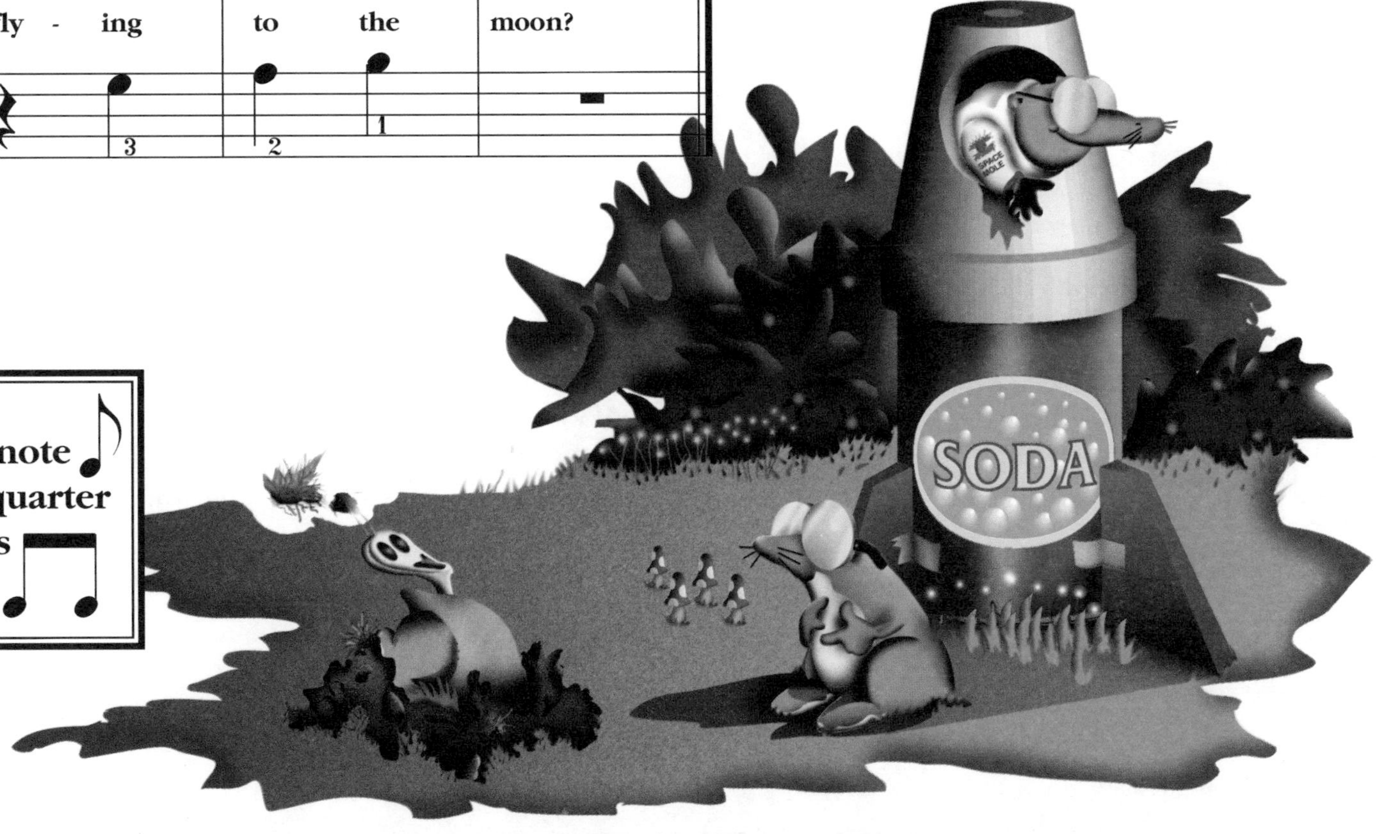

SODA

The time value of an eighth note ♪ is HALF as long as that of a quarter note. Play TWO eighth notes to ONE count.

PAPA HAYDN", as Mozart lovingly called this great musician, inherited his sense of humor and genius from his father, Mathias Haydn, who was a hard-working and jolly man. He lived in Rohrau, a small Austrian village where, in a combination shop and home, he made and repaired wheels. He had a fine tenor voice and was the sexton and organist in the village church. His wife sang in the choir.

Young Joseph had eleven brothers and sisters. At the age of 5 he was taken to a nearby village where he was taught music. He was always full of mischief and one day as a result of a prank, he was turned out into the stormy night—homeless.

The following morning, he went to a friend, a wigmaker and barber, who let him use his garret. Here, on a dilapidated harpsichord, with snow blowing through the cracks of the roof, Joseph worked and studied.

On moonlight nights he and his friends used to stroll about the streets of Vienna serenading famous musicians. After years of hard work he wrote some of the most magnificent compositions known.

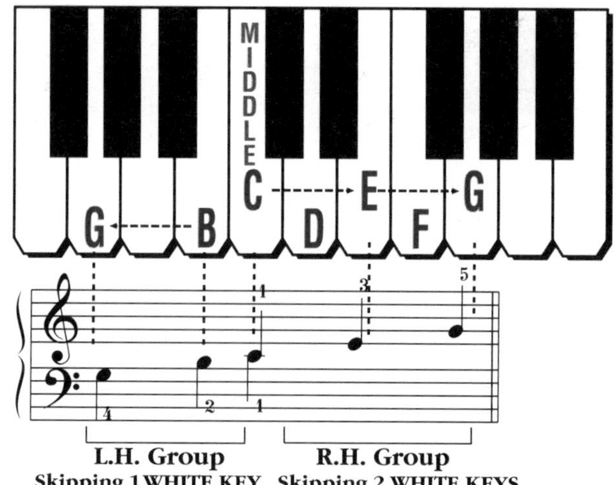
MIDDLE C
G B C D E F G
L.H. Group
Skipping 1 WHITE KEY
R.H. Group
Skipping 2 WHITE KEYS

Air

(from Surprise Symphony)

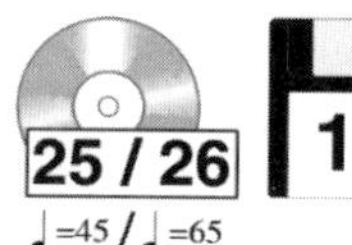
25 / 26
13

♩=45 / ♩=65

Pa - pa Hay-dn's dead and gone, But his mem'-ry lin-gers on;

When his mood was one of bliss, He wrote jol - ly tunes like this.

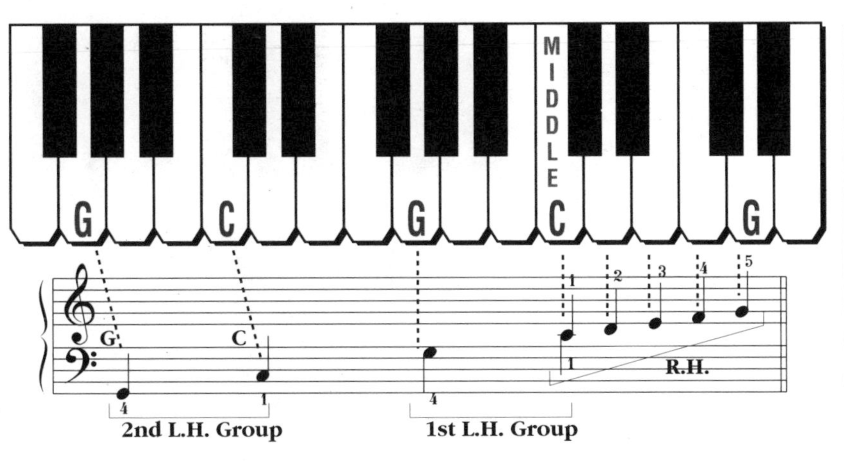
M I D D L E
G
C
G
C
G
G
C
R.H.
2nd L.H. Group
1st L.H. Group

PREPARATION
LOCATE, NAME and PLAY the THREE G's.

LOCATE, NAME and PLAY the TWO C's.

Play and name the first L.H. group, then the second L.H. group and the R.H. group.

By the Pond

27 / 28
♩=55 / ♩=75

14

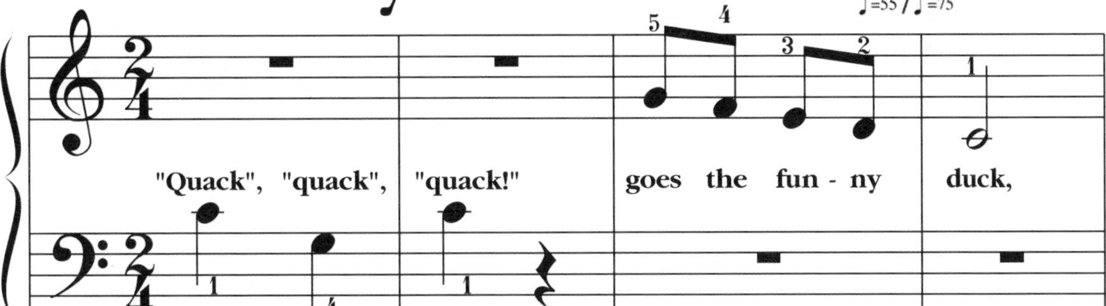
"Quack", "quack", "quack!" goes the fun - ny duck,

"Croak", "croak", "croak!" goes the frog - gie too.

BUBBLE
GUM

Always
Be
Curious
to find other F♯
BLACK keys on the piano.

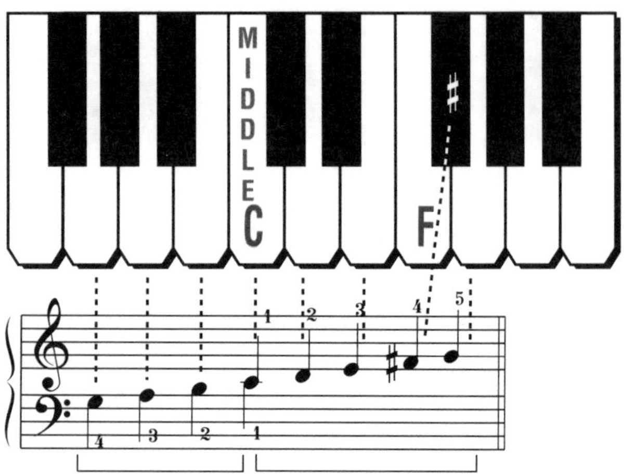
MIDDLE C
F
♯

L.H. Group R.H. Group - Note BLACK KEY

This sign ♯ is called a SHARP. In this piece you will see it in the first and fifth measures in front of F.
It means to play the BLACK key to the right of F instead of the white key F.

Paper Ships

29 / 30
♩=65 / ♩=85

15

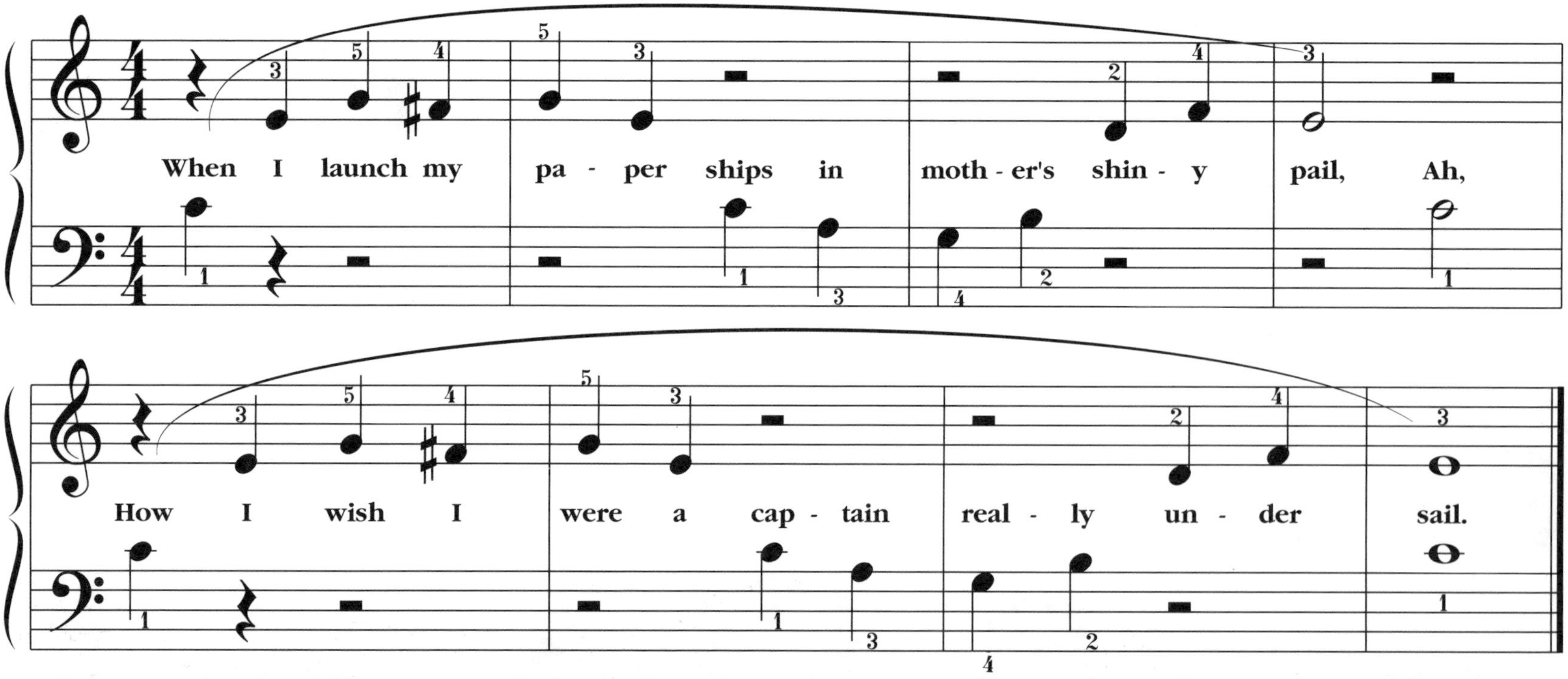

When I launch my pa - per ships in moth - er's shin - y pail, Ah,

How I wish I were a cap - tain real - ly un - der sail.

Sledding

When the SHARP sign ♯ is placed between the Clef sign and the time signature it becomes the KEY SIGNATURE. In this piece ALL F's must be sharped — *played on **BLACK** key F.*
31 / 32
♩=70 / ♩=90
16
Snow - flakes fall - ing fluff - y and white;
O, what fun! We're sled - ding to - night.

Note: — This piece contains the SCALE OF G MAJOR. Those who desire to introduce scales at this stage of instruction may have their pupils make good use of "PETER'S BLANK MUSIC BOOK" (wide ruling).

The Butterfly

33 / 34 17

♩=80 / ♩=100

But - ter - fly bright in the sun - light,

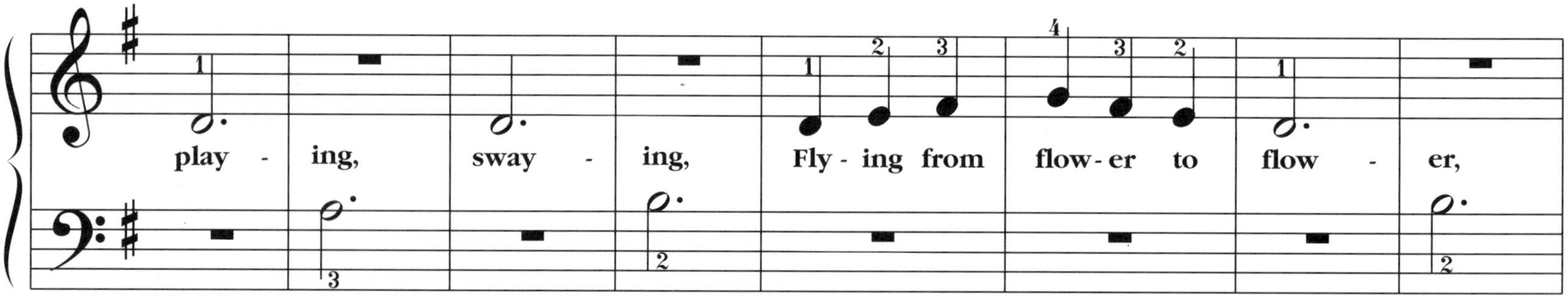

play - ing, sway - ing, Fly - ing from flow - er to flow - er,

blithe
and
gay.

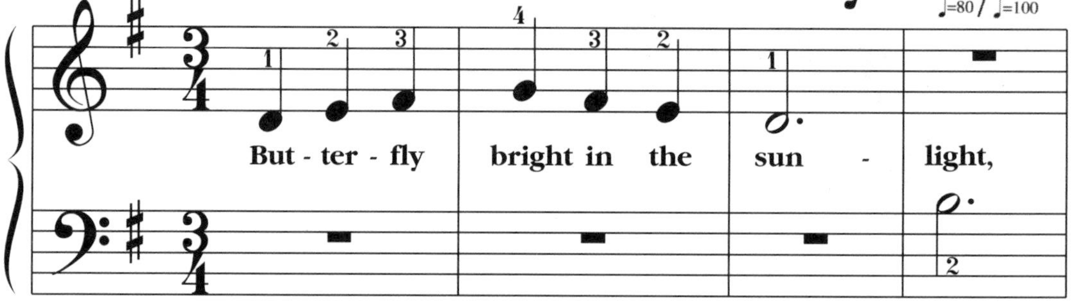

THE TIE

The TIE is a curved line joining one note to another of the SAME PITCH and means that the second note is to be held *for its full value without being struck.*

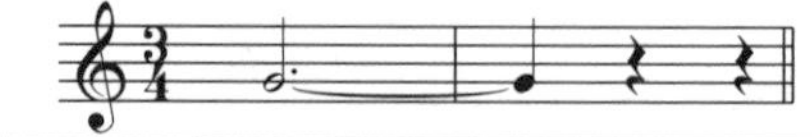

PREPARATION
Locate, name and play the L.H. Group and then the R.H. Group

C D E MIDDLE C C D E
C D E
3 2 1
1 2 3
C D E
L.H. Group
R.H. Group
Questions
35 / 36
♩=80 / ♩=100
18
Dwarf
1 2
"Gi - ant, why are you so tall?"
Giant
"Well, sir, why are you so small?"
3 2 1 2

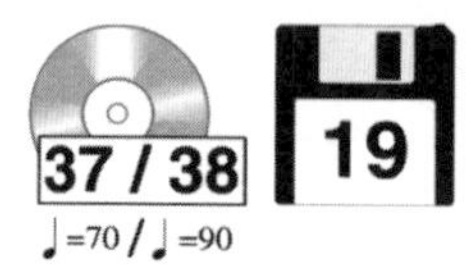
37 / 38
19
♩=70 / ♩=90

MIDDLE C
♯
C♯ (Sharp)

Look and listen for **Black** Middle C

Blue-Bells of Scotland

O where, and O where is your High-land lad-die gone? O where, and O where is your High-land lad-die gone? He's gone to fight the foe for King George up-on the throne; And it's Oh! in my heart, I wish him safe at home!

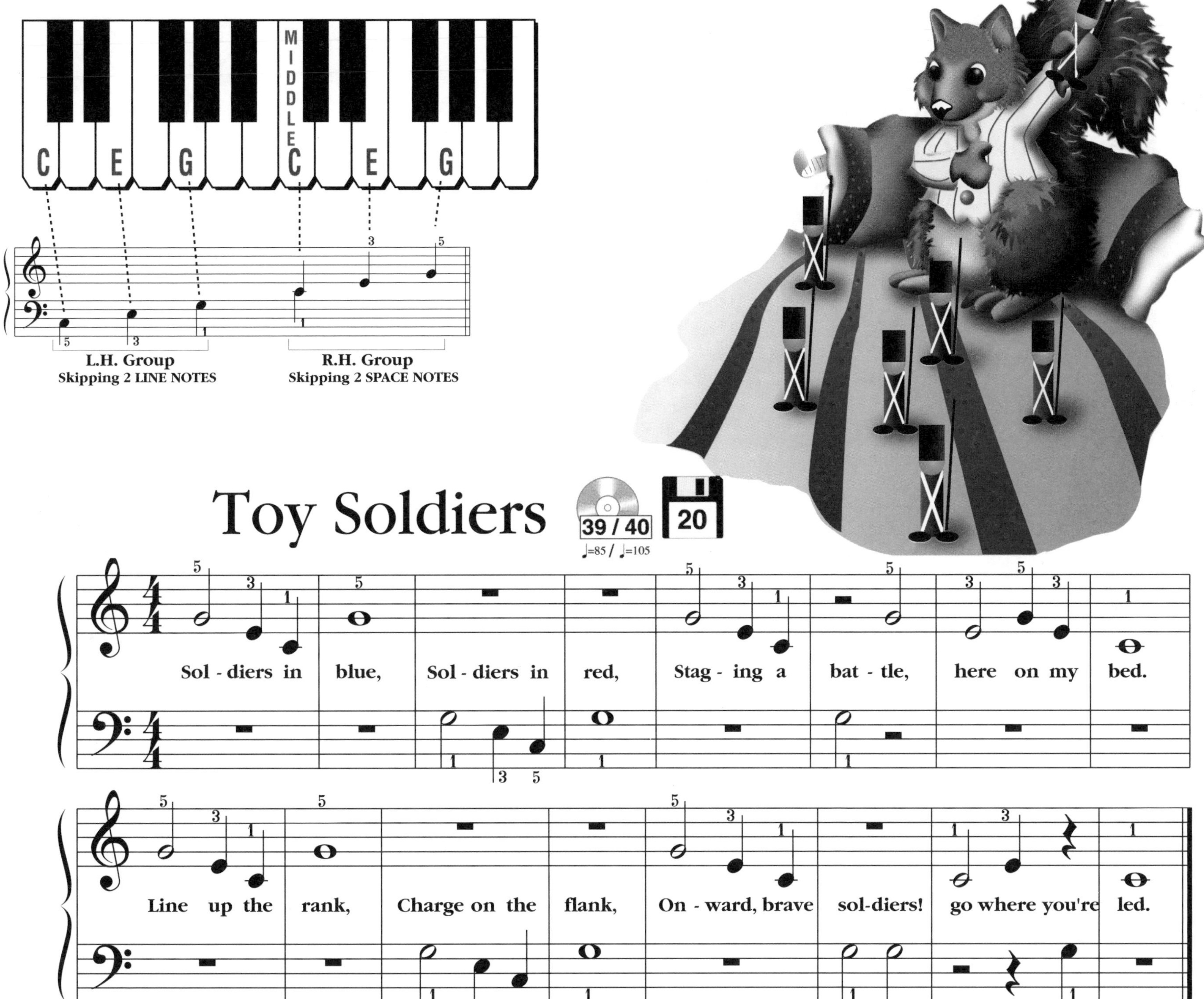
MIDDLE C
C
E
G
C
E
G
L.H. Group
Skipping 2 LINE NOTES
R.H. Group
Skipping 2 SPACE NOTES
Toy Soldiers
39 / 40
20
♩=85 / ♩=105
Sol - diers in
blue,
Sol - diers in
red,
Stag - ing a
bat - tle,
here on my
bed.
Line up the
rank,
Charge on the
flank,
On - ward, brave
sol-diers!
go where you're
led.

OLD SALT
Tea Bags
OLD SALT
Tea Bags
Big Ships
41 / 42
♩=80 / ♩=100
21
I see the big ships a - sail - ing
O - ver the pret - ty blue sea,
I'd like to know where they're go - ing,
But they will nev - er tell me.

Always
Be
Careful
to look and listen for the FLAT, SHARP, and NATURAL

This ♭ is the **BLACK** key sign called FLAT. It means that you must play the first **BLACK** key to the LEFT of the white key **A** in this piece.

This ♮ sign is a NATURAL which means that when you see it in front of a note that has been played on a **BLACK** key you must play it on its NATURAL, the white key.

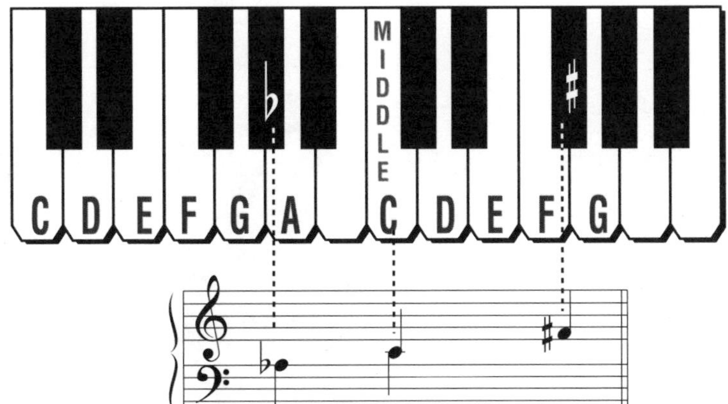
MIDDLE
C D E F G A C D E F G

43 / 44
♩=65 / ♩=85
22

Steam-boat Round the Bend

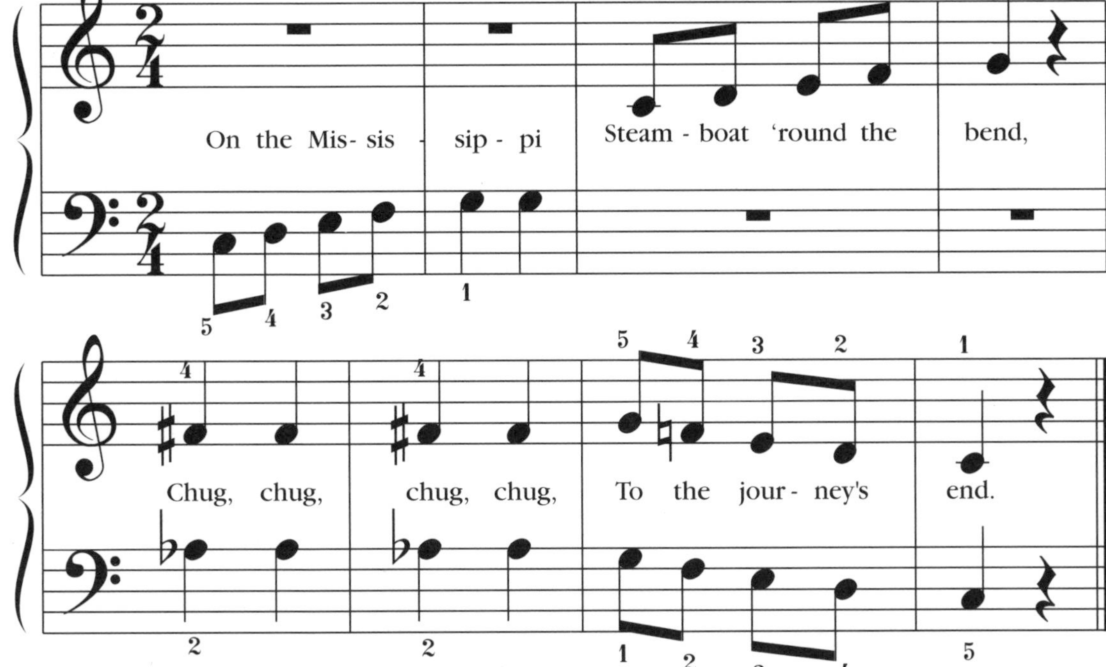
On the Mis- sis - sip - pi
Steam - boat 'round the bend,
Chug, chug, chug, chug,
To the jour - ney's end.

S.S. OTTER

Comin' Round the Mountain

SECONDO

(For Teacher or Slightly Advanced Pupil)

As lively as possible
sempre stacc.
Repeat ad lib.

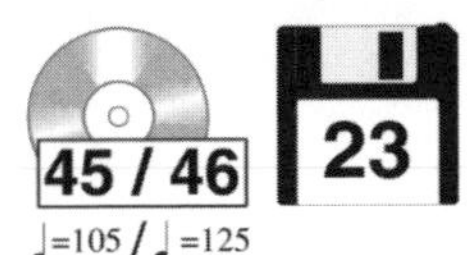
45 / 46
♩=105 / ♩=125
23

Comin' Round the Mountain

PRIMO

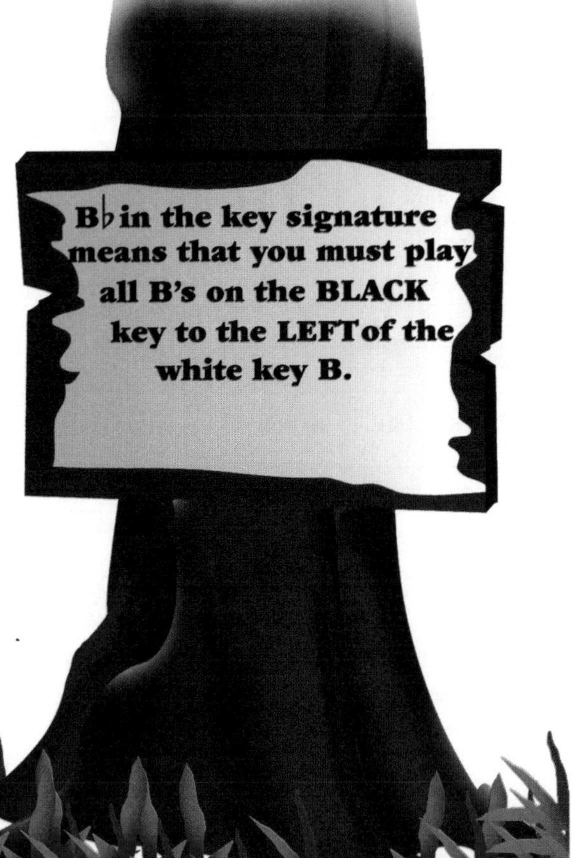
B♭ in the key signature means that you must play all B's on the BLACK key to the LEFT of the white key B.

As lively as possible

Southern Mountain Song

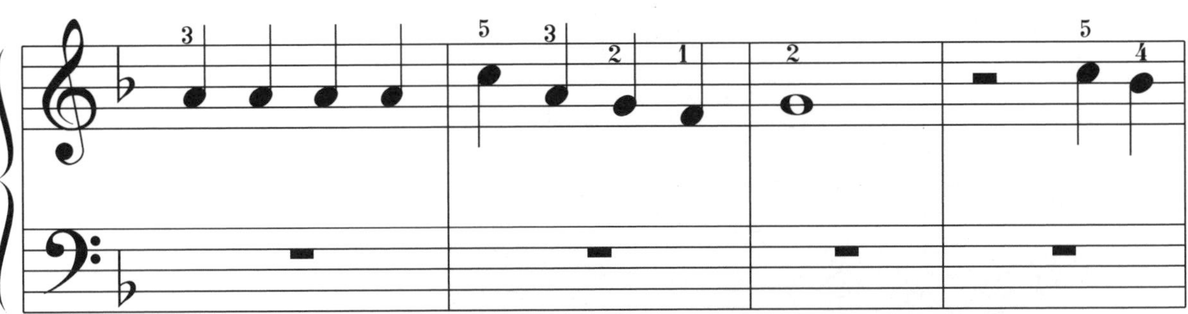

Repeat ad lib.

L.H.
L.H.

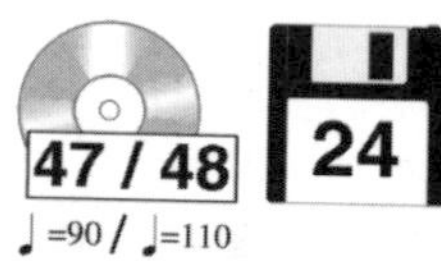

47 / 48
♩=90 / ♩=110
24

The Long Trail

R.H.
Hik-ing the trails of the Rock - ies,
L.H. over

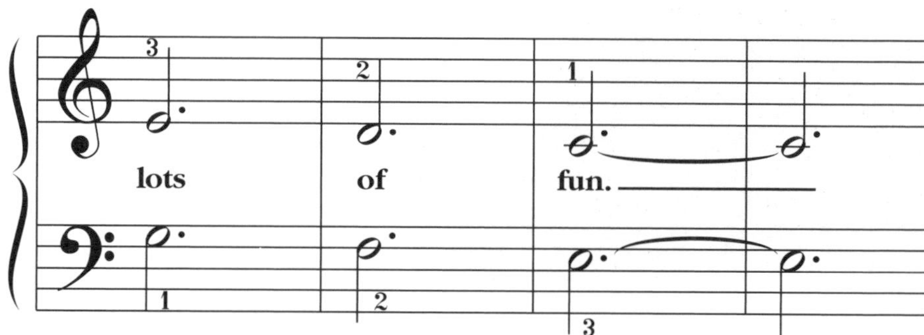

lots of fun.

R.H.
Climb-ing up hill ver - y slow - ly, come down on the run.
L.H. over

NO
TRESPASSING

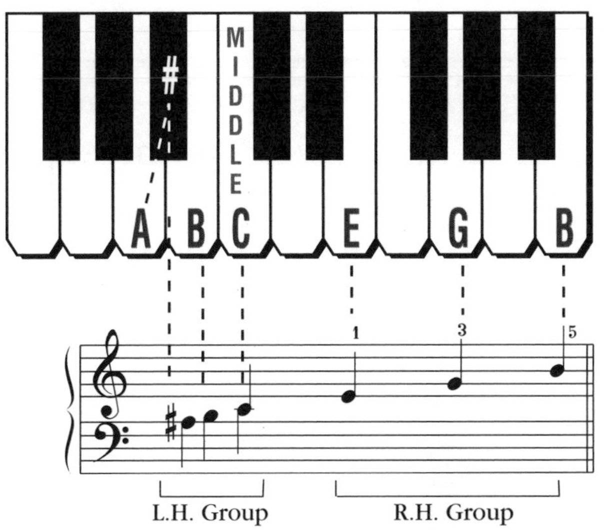
MIDDLE
#
A
B
C
E
G
B
L.H. Group
R.H. Group

49 / 50
♩=63 / ♩=83

25

"A" SHARP is the first BLACK KEY to the Right of A

Skipping SPACE notes F and A

The Bee

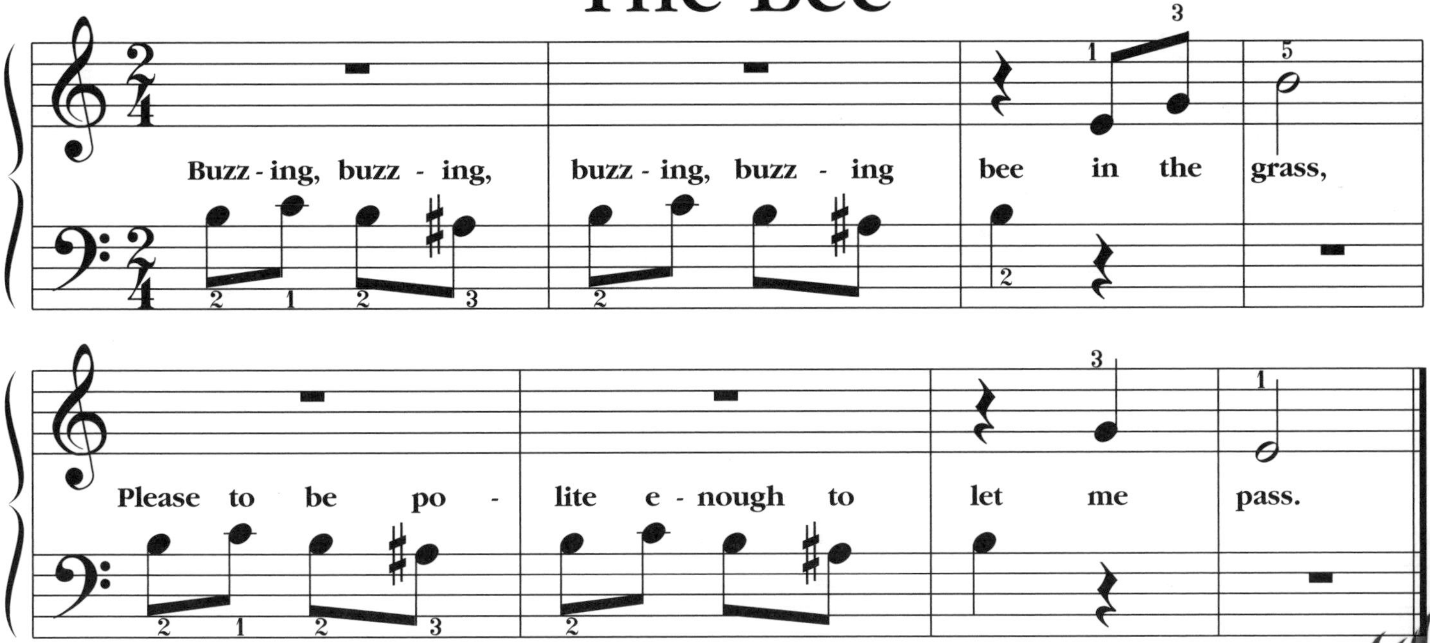

Buzz - ing, buzz - ing, buzz - ing, buzz - ing bee in the grass,

Please to be po - lite e - nough to let me pass.

This piece begins on a weak beat—the last count in a measure. You must therefore ACCENT the first beat after the bar line. The missing counts of the first measure will be found in the last measure of the piece.

My Bonnie

51 / 52
♩=80 / ♩=100
26

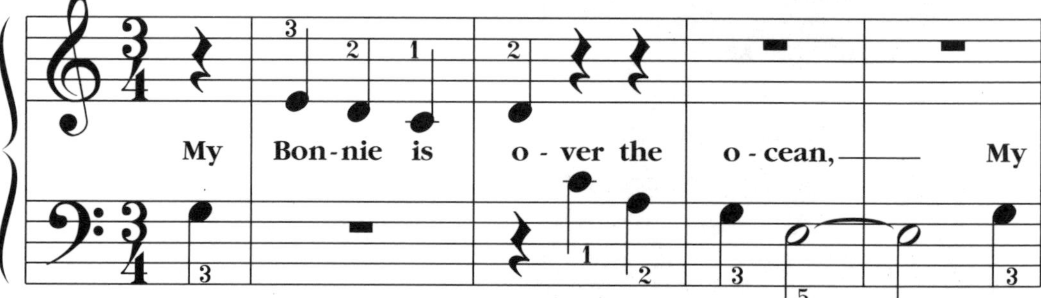
My Bon-nie is o - ver the o - cean, My

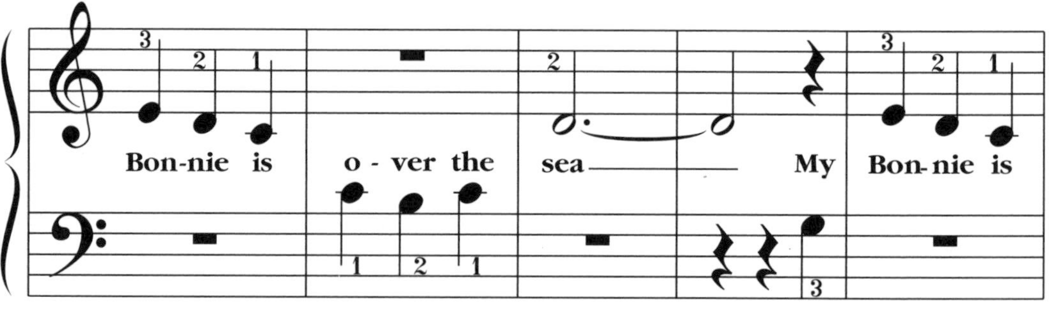
Bon-nie is o - ver the sea My Bon-nie is

o - ver the o - cean, Oh bring back my Bon - nie to me.

8······ means: Play EIGHT keys higher

Vacation Time

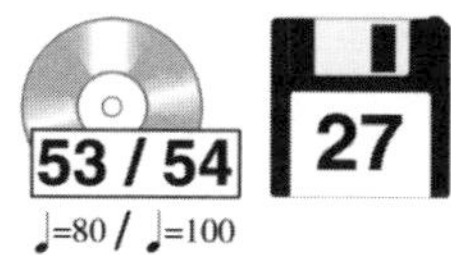
53 / 54
27
♩=80 / ♩=100

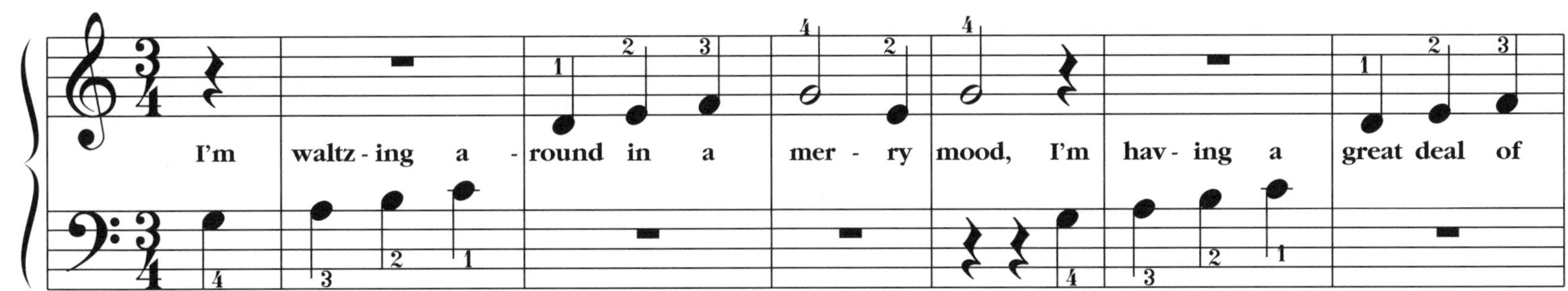
I'm waltz - ing a - round in a mer - ry mood, I'm hav - ing a great deal of

fun, There's nev - er a cloud in the sky to - day, Va -

8

ca - tion has be - gun.

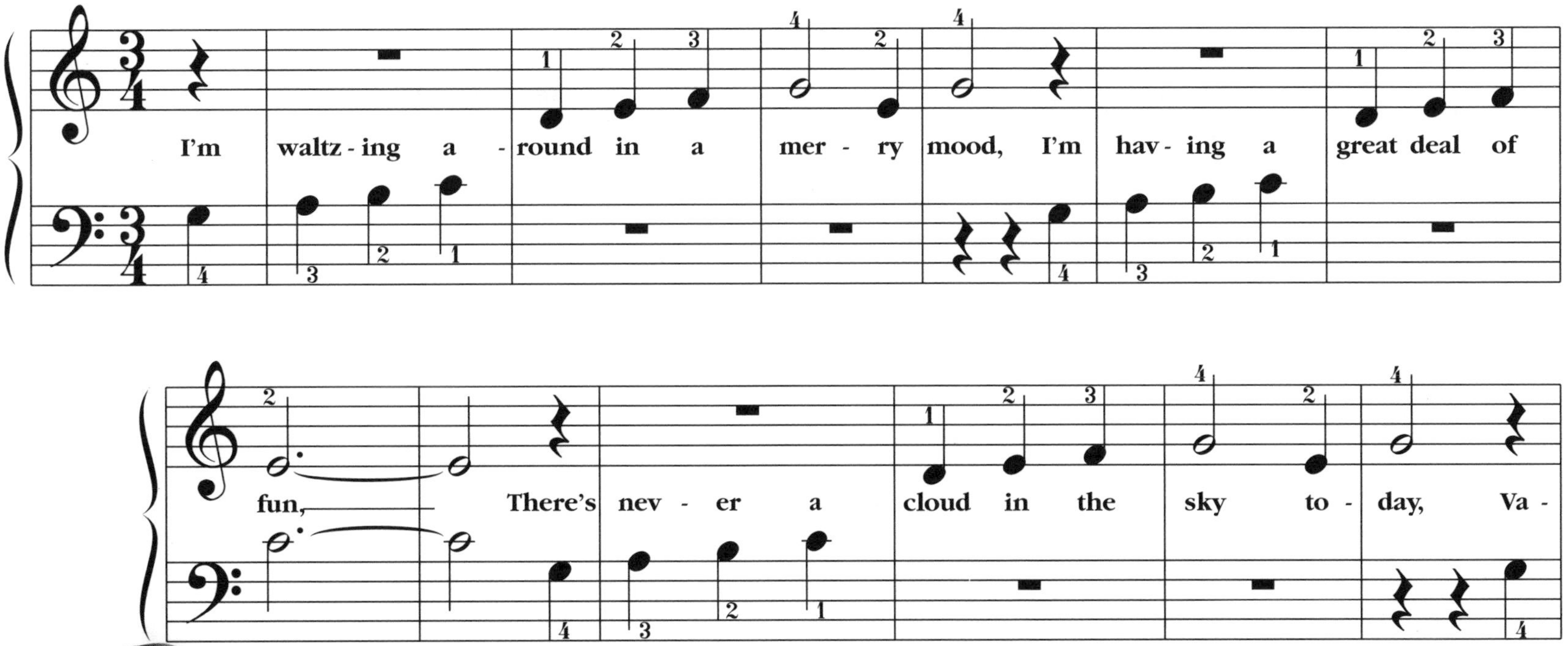

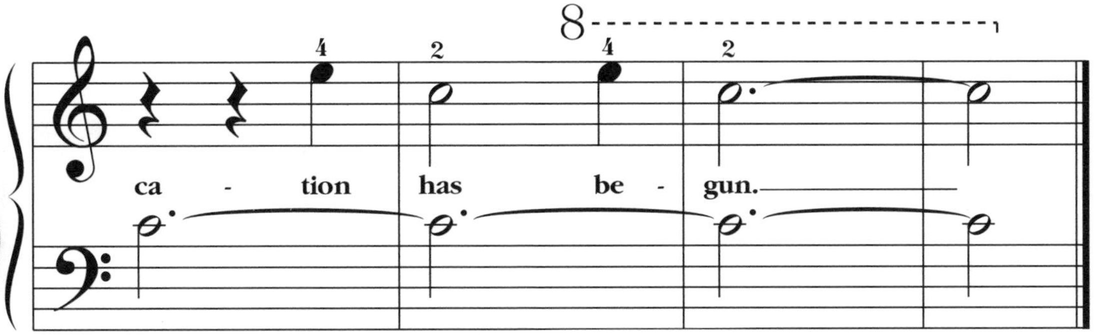

Home on the Range

SECONDO

Slowly with much expression

Teacher or slightly advanced pupil

Cowboy Ballad

A
B
C
D
Fine
Refrain
E
F
D.S. al Fine

Home on the Range

55 / 56
28

PRIMO

Slowly with much expression

Cowboy Ballad

Oh, give me a home where the buf-fa-lo roam, Where deer and an-te-lope play, Where

sel-dom is heard a dis-cour-ag-ing word, And skies are not cloud-y all day.

Fine

Home, home on the range; The deer and the an-te-lope play, Where

D.S. al Fine

D.S. al Fine-go back to the 𝄋 sign and play until the **Fine.**

The Juggler

57 / 58 ♩=60 / ♩=80 29

Jug - gler, Jug - gler, what's your name?

L.H. over L.H. over

All the cir-cus post-ers ad-ver-tise your fame!

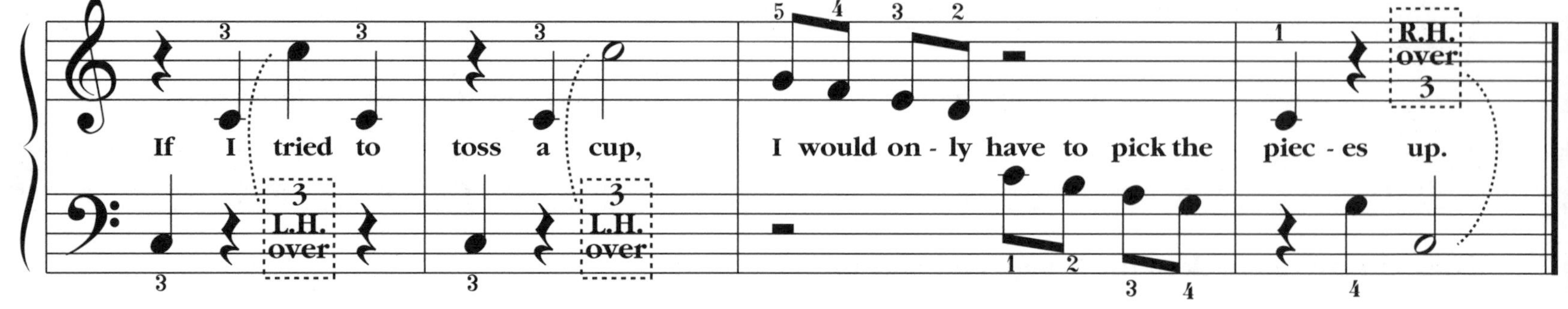
If I tried to toss a cup,
I would on - ly have to pick the piec - es up.
L.H. over
L.H. over
R.H. over

C
E
F
G
MIDDLE C
E
G
Together
Play both keys together
R.H. Group.
E♭ is the 1st BLACK key to the LEFT of E.
59 / 60
30
♩=75 / ♩=95

From a Wigwam

CERTIFICATE of MERIT

This certifies that

....

has successfully completed

TEACHING LITTLE FINGERS TO PLAY

and is eligible for promotion to

"TEACHING LITTLE FINGERS TO PLAY MORE"

....

Teacher

....

Date

Cut Certificate out on Dotted line